THE MONSTER
Written and drawn by

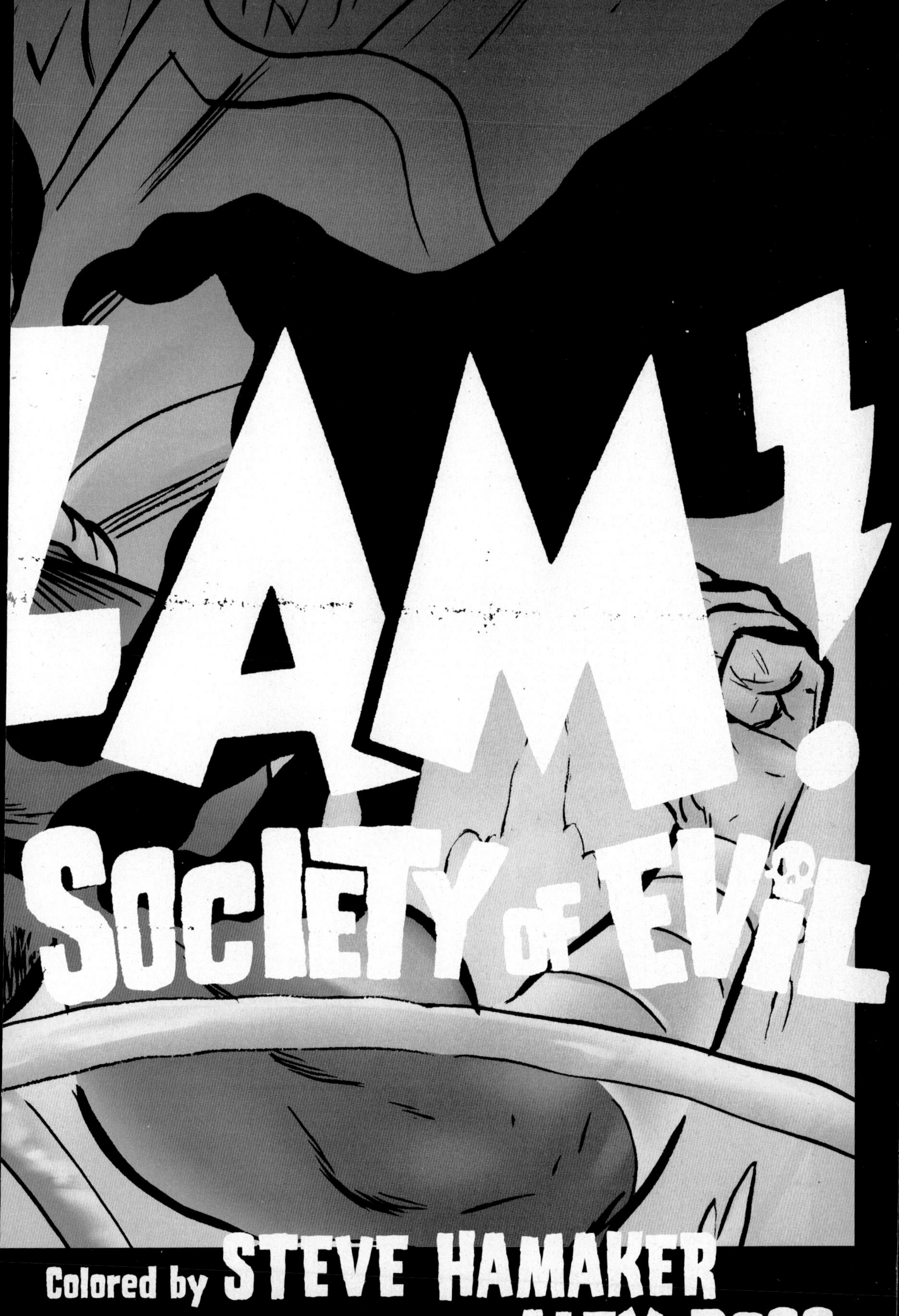

Colored by **STEVE HAMAKER**

Introduction by **ALEX ROSS**

Cover art by Jeff Smith with Steve Hamaker

 DC Comics, 1700 Broadway, New York, NY 10019. A Warner Bros. Entertainment Company. Printed in Canada. First Printing. ISBN:978-1-4012-0974-2

SFI CERTIFIED SOURCING
Fiber used in this product line meets the sourcing requirements of the SFI program.
www.sfiprogram.org
PWC-SFICOC-260

Introduction by Alex Ross

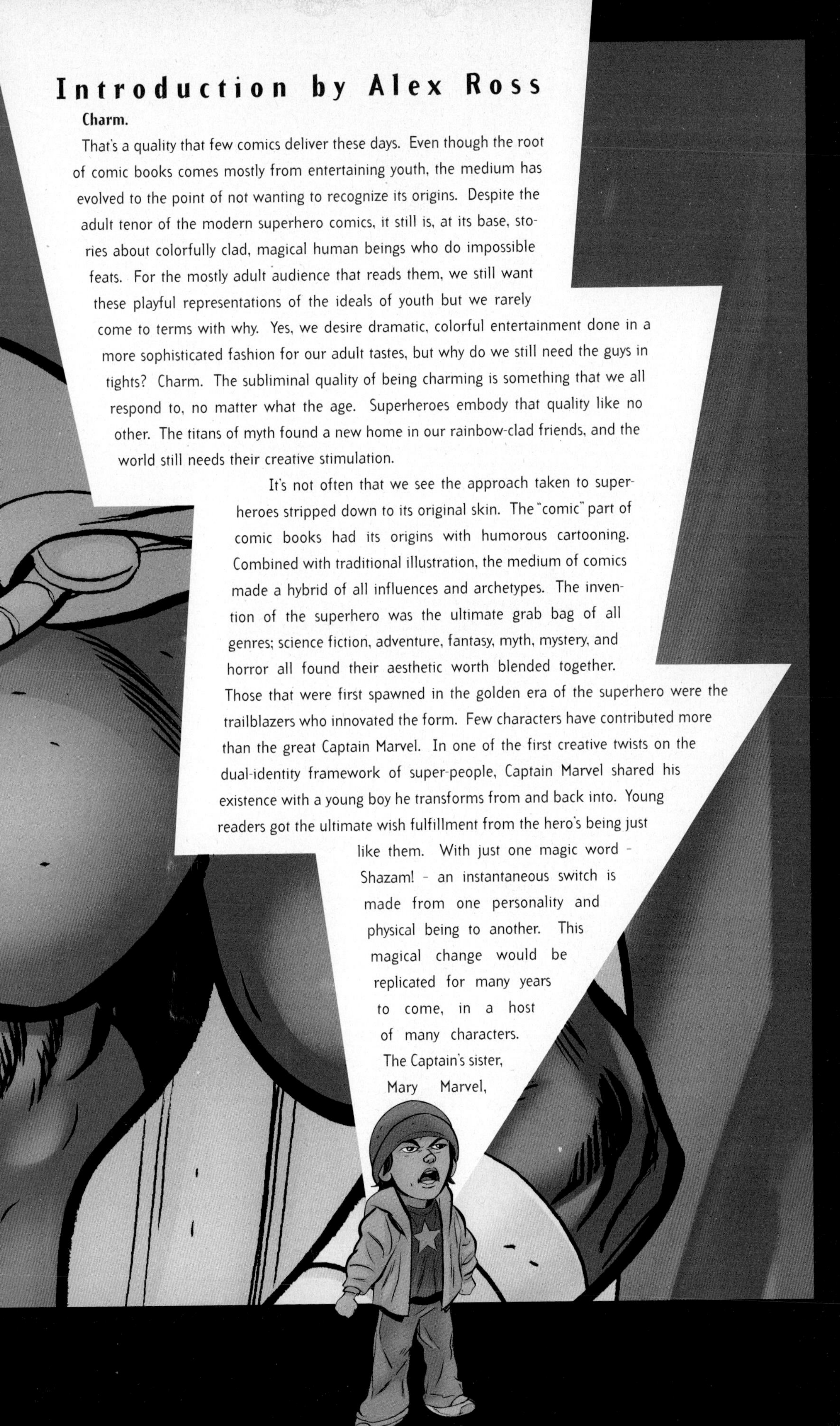

Charm.

That's a quality that few comics deliver these days. Even though the root of comic books comes mostly from entertaining youth, the medium has evolved to the point of not wanting to recognize its origins. Despite the adult tenor of the modern superhero comics, it still is, at its base, stories about colorfully clad, magical human beings who do impossible feats. For the mostly adult audience that reads them, we still want these playful representations of the ideals of youth but we rarely come to terms with why. Yes, we desire dramatic, colorful entertainment done in a more sophisticated fashion for our adult tastes, but why do we still need the guys in tights? Charm. The subliminal quality of being charming is something that we all respond to, no matter what the age. Superheroes embody that quality like no other. The titans of myth found a new home in our rainbow-clad friends, and the world still needs their creative stimulation.

It's not often that we see the approach taken to superheroes stripped down to its original skin. The "comic" part of comic books had its origins with humorous cartooning. Combined with traditional illustration, the medium of comics made a hybrid of all influences and archetypes. The invention of the superhero was the ultimate grab bag of all genres; science fiction, adventure, fantasy, myth, mystery, and horror all found their aesthetic worth blended together. Those that were first spawned in the golden era of the superhero were the trailblazers who innovated the form. Few characters have contributed more than the great Captain Marvel. In one of the first creative twists on the dual-identity framework of super-people, Captain Marvel shared his existence with a young boy he transforms from and back into. Young readers got the ultimate wish fulfillment from the hero's being just like them. With just one magic word – Shazam! – an instantaneous switch is made from one personality and physical being to another. This magical change would be replicated for many years to come, in a host of many characters. The Captain's sister, Mary Marvel, of young girls empowered like the boys. The bald scientist villain, Sivana, and the numerous other villains the Marvel Family would face, had more creative juices flowing into the bloodstream of comics. Behind all of this was the talented team of artist C.C. Beck and writer Otto Binder. The greatest asset of their talents was the childlike whimsy their comics captured, perfectly crafted for the audience they knew well.

Beck's art style kept a strong link to comics' humorous cartooning roots, existing in somewhat of its own hybrid landscape of realism and fable. Binder kept that same bridge between the unfettered imagination of youth and the maturity of the modern world. Captain Marvel's prime period of impact was during the Second World War, where he provided entertainment of juvenile distraction and simultaneously directed attention to the war effort. His effect was felt far beyond the shores of America, as he served to inspire readers in a growing international comics market.

Today in comics the divide between the whimsy of cartoon entertainment and realistic illustrated fare has never been more separate. Most often it doesn't attempt to bridge the two, keeping the medium a ghettoized environment. Jeff Smith is one of the only people to challenge that separation and successfully hurdle its boundaries. The amazing accomplishment of his "Bone" saga, done over the last several years, truly recaptured a seemingly lost quality in comics. The mixing of animation-style rendering with whimsical characters wandering into an epic fantasy created one of the most charming comics in decades. Jeff also self-published from the start, making his mark in the comic book field on his own terms. As well, the character of Bone and his accompanying mythos is one that Jeff brought up through his childhood into the published reality of adulthood. His story is truly one to be an inspiration to us all.

Jeff's first project since "Bone" is this new use of Captain Marvel and his cast of characters, delighting Shazam fans like myself that an approach like presentation. He didn't disappoint, as Jeff returned to the roots of this superhero's magic, finding that balance between the child and man. Retelling the Marvel Family's story from the beginning with an eye for detail often forgotten from his origins, both in tone and art, the story innovates further by melding that with a modern sensibility. Jeff's interpretation of Billy Batson as a tiny boy adds so much to the magic wish fulfillment of the story. Truly spending time with an all-too-young homeless orphan regained an important perspective on this character. The gentle care Jeff takes to tell his story is a welcome shock from comics' more standard storytelling approach.

I had the privilege of seeing the book's progress at a point when Jeff came through Chicago, where I saw the lengths he took to realize Captain Marvel's feline friend Tawky Tawny as a true tiger. Knowing that Jeff was revitalizing this character to his original state with a slight spin was purely inspiring. And, frankly, nothing is cuter than seeing Mary Marvel represented as a little tiny girl, impishly accompanying her "big" brother.

I must also say I'm grateful for the creative contribution to Captain Marvel's personal definition Jeff gave. For many years, the standard approach to his character has been that he was simply a boy inside a man's body. Jeff knew the original concept to his characterization was much more than that. Bringing back the quality of how Captain Marvel was much like a genie inside Billy Batson's bottle, with some distinction of minds and maturity, was a welcome change.

Jeff approached this story with great passion and purpose, not just to provide his perspective on a legend but to make a metaphor for our times. It's no accident the book has a post 9-11 haunting feel to it.

Jeff's creativity and contribution to comics is worthy of great attention and celebration. Inspiring like his work, he's also one of the nicest people you could ever meet. I'm proud to know him. Thanks for the great Shazam book, Jeff!

THE MONSTER SOCIETY OF EVIL

CHAPTER 1:

YROOB SZH Z HVXIVG!*

*THE MONSTER SOCIETY CODE

A	B	C	D	E	F	G	H	I	J	K	L	M	N	O	P	Q	R	S	T	U	V	W	X	Y	Z
Z	Y	X	W	V	U	T	S	R	Q	P	O	N	M	L	K	J	I	H	G	F	E	D	C	B	A

KRAK!
WAREHOUSE
BA-BOOM!

JUST WEEKS AFTER LOSING THE ELECTION TO HIS DEAD OPPONENT'S WIFE . . .

. . . IT LOOKS LIKE THE FORMER INDUSTRIALIST'S POLITICAL CAREER HAS BEEN **SAVED.** CONFIRMATION HEARINGS FOR THE NEW **ATTORNEY GENERAL** HAVE BEEN FASTER THAN EXPECTED.
UP NEXT: THE **WEATHER** - - IT'S GOING TO BE A COLD ONE AGAIN.

HEY!

GO ON - - Shoo!
YOU DON'T WANT TO BE AROUND ME.
NOBODY DOES.

BAM! BAM! BAM!

CLICK!

I KNOW YOU'RE **IN THERE**, KID. YOU'RE NOT SUPPOSED TO BE IN THIS BUILDING!

C'MON, LET ME IN. I JUST NEED A LITTLE **CASH** . . .
I KNOW YOU GOT SOME.
BAM!
ERK!

I'VE SEEN THAT OLD BUM DOWN BY THE RIVER GIVE YOU MONEY.

DAMMIT! YOU GOT THIS DOOR **NAILED SHUT?**
BAM!

SCRAPE

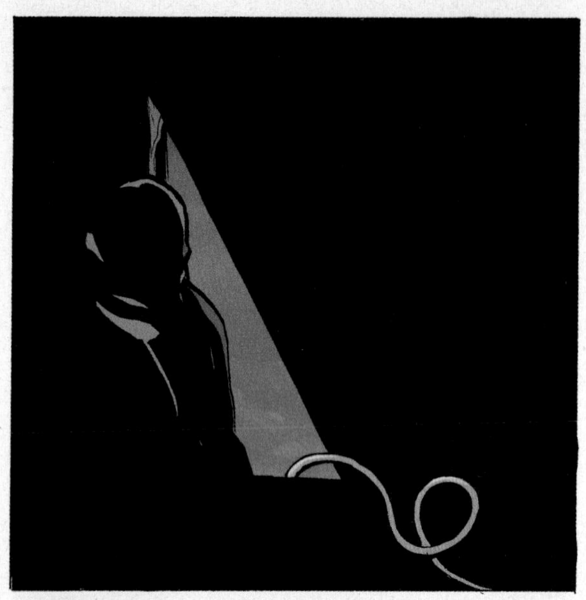

KRAKKABOOM!

DON'T MESS WITH ME, KID.
HUFF! HUFF!

ANY MONEY YOU GOT BELONGS TO ME . . .

YOU WANNA LIVE ON THE STREET, YOU GOTTA LEARN THE **RULES.**

RULE NUMBER ONE: I'M **BIGGER** THAN YOU!
OW!
DON'T!

YOU'RE GONNA LEARN **RESPECT** - -
STOP!
STOP!

'CAUSE I'M GONNA **TEACH YOU . . .**

FEAR!

HOW'S YOUR SOUP, BILLY?
...

IT'S GOOD AND IT'S **REAL HOT!**
I BROUGHT YOUR CHANGE. YOU WANT TO COUNT IT?

NO, NO, YOU KEEP IT! IT IS YOUR **TIP** FOR RUNNING ERRANDS FOR ME.
BUT ALL I DID WAS PICK UP A FEW GROCERIES. ARE YOU **SURE?**
...

YOU KNOW HOW HARD IT IS FOR ME TO GO INTO THE CITY, BILLY. IT HELPS WHEN YOU DO IT.
WOW! THANKS, TALKY! I WOULDN'T KNOW WHAT TO DO WITHOUT YOU.

RAIN'S COMIN'. . . I CAN FEEL IT IN MY HIP. COLD, **WINTER** RAIN.

THAT'S NOT GOOD FOR PEOPLE LIKE US.
...

YOU KNOW, BILLY, LIVING THIS WAY - - OUTSIDE IN THE COLD - - IS ALL RIGHT FOR ME, I'M A **WANDERER**. I CHOSE THIS LIFE A LONG TIME AGO . . . BUT **YOU** DO NOT DESERVE THIS.
...

YOU ARE A GOOD KID WITH BAD LUCK. WHY DON'T YOU GO DOWN TO THE SHELTER? THEY CAN HELP YOU . . .
I DON'T LIKE THE SHELTER.

FOR ONE THING, THEY WON'T LET ME HANG OUT WITH YOU - -
HEY!
WHO'S THAT?

WHERE?
THAT GUY ACROSS THE STREET - - DON'T YOU SEE HIM?

I DON'T SEE ANYONE - -
YOU DON'T?
HE LOOKS JUST LIKE MY DAD.
MY **REAL** DAD.

NOW, HONEY, YOU KNOW THAT CAN'T BE.
BUT IT LOOKS JUST LIKE HIM!

Subway

Subwa

CLOSED

Downtown
3

WHERE DID HE GO?
3
CLICKETY CLAK!

TOOOO-OOT!
TOOT!
CLACKETY CLICK!

SCREEEEEEEEEEECH!

PSHT!

CLICK! CLICK! CLICK!
DAD?

PSSHT!

CHUNK!
CLICKETY CLACK! CLICKETY CLACK!
WHERE ARE WE GOING?

CLICKETY CLACK! CLICKETY CLACK! CLICKETY CLACK! CLICKETY

SCREEEEEEEEEECH!

PSSHT!

GET OFF.

AREN'T YOU COMING WITH ME?
PSHT!

CLICKETY CLACK!

HOLY MOLEY.

PRIDE
ENVY
GREED

HATRED
SELFISHNESS
LAZINESS
INJUSTICE

OH, BOY.

BILLY BATSON, COME HERE.

RIDE
ENVY
GREED

ARE YOU GOD?

OF COURSE NOT. I AM AS MORTAL AS YOU ARE. WHAT I **AM** IS A **WIZARD**.
NOW GET UP. YOU DON'T BOW BEFORE WIZARDS.

SORRY. HOW DO YOU KNOW MY NAME?

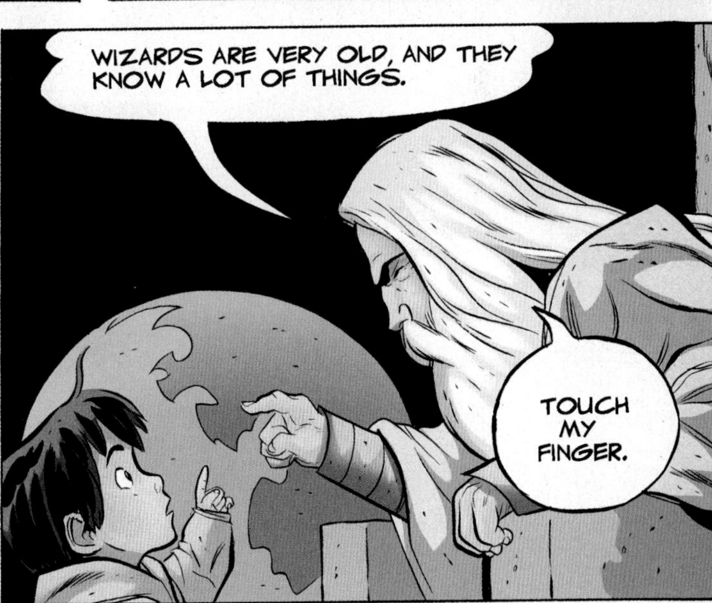
WIZARDS ARE VERY OLD, AND THEY KNOW A LOT OF THINGS.
TOUCH MY FINGER.

SNAP!

YES, YOU'LL DO NICELY.

WHY DID YOU DO THAT?

I WANTED TO SEE IF YOU WERE FILLED WITH GOOD ELECTRICITY.
YOU ARE.
YOU SEE, BILLY...

THERE ARE MANY FORCES IN THE WORLD. SOME ARE GOOD, AND OTHERS ARE LESS SO...
SELFISHNESS
LAZINESS
INJUSTICE

IT HAS ALWAYS BEEN MY JOB TO BATTLE THE DARKER FORCES, AND DOWN THROUGH THE AGES, IN EVERY CIVILIZATION, I HAVE DONE SO...

BUT I AM GETTING OLD, BILLY BATSON, AND IT IS TIME FOR ME TO PICK A REPLACEMENT.

SAY THE MAGIC WORD!

BABOO

ZZT
ZZT
ZZT.

HELLO, MARVEL.

MASTER, I FEEL STRANGE.
YOU HAVE A NEW HOST. A YOUNG BOY NAMED **BILLY BATSON.**
HE IS A GOOD BOY, YOU'LL LIKE HIM.

I DON'T
INDERSTAND - -
MY TIME ON THIS PLANE IS NEARLY OVER . . .
DO YOU SEE THE STONE ABOVE ME?

ZZT!
ZZT!

MASTER! IT HANGS BY A THREAD! DON'T SIT THERE!
STAY BACK!

IF YOU MUST CONTACT ME, LIGHT TH
BRAZIER. NOW SAY THE MAGIC WORD AND RESTORE THE BOY.

SHAZAM.

BOOM

MMM...MM...

shazam...

BABOOM!
I KNOW THAT KID HAS MONEY STASHED AWAY **SOMEWHERE** - -
CLINK!
ARE YOU STILL HERE?

YOU STILL **AWAKE?**
I'M GONNA HAVE TO STOMP YOU **AGAIN!**

EENH!

OW!
HEY!

YOU BRAT!
YOU TRYIN'
JUDO ON ME---

HMMM.

THIS IS NO WAY FOR A KID TO LIVE.

CLICK!
--THE NEW ATTORNEY GENERAL OF THE UNITED STATES IS SCHEDULED TO MAKE HIS FIRST PRESS CONFERENCE LATER TODAY--

WHEW!

HEY!
THERE YOU ARE! I KNEW YOU'D COME OUT SOONER OR LATER!

CIRCUS
GET BACK HERE!

SCREEECH!
HONK! HONK!

TAXI

HOT DOGS

HELP YOU?
YEAH! I WANT TO BUY A HOT DOG FOR A FRIEND --
HOT DOGS

WHAT DO YOU WANT ON IT?
IT'S NOT FOR ME, IT'S FOR MY **FRIEND.** HE'LL TELL YOU WHAT HE WANTS WHEN HE GETS HERE.
HIS NAME IS CAPTAIN MARVEL!
HOT DOGS

HERE! JUST TAKE IT!
HOT DOGS

RRR! WHERE'S THAT **KID?!**

WHAT DO YOU WANT ON --
KEERAK
BOOM!!

HEY, THAT WAS CLOSE! LIGHTNING MUST'VE HIT INSIDE THE PARK!
THANKS FOR THE CHOW.
HEH, HEH!

SEE YOU AROUND, OLD MAN - -
THUD!

I BELIEVE THIS IS MINE, LAGREEN!
HOW DO YOU KNOW MY NAME?

THIS IS YOUR LAST WARNING.
STAY AWAY FROM ME!!

HE'S A THIEF WHO PREYS ON HOMELESS CHILDREN.

AND YOU PROTECT THEM - - FOR HOT DOGS?
NO, BUT I LIKE HOT DOGS, AND I DO NOT HAVE ANY OF MY OWN MONEY.
COULD I HAVE MUSTARD AND ONIONS ON THIS, PLEASE?

DON'T YOU HAVE THE ONIONS IN THE TOMATO SAUCE? NO? THAT'S ALL RIGHT.

MMM . . . YOU KNOW, I THINK OF ALL THE ADVANCEMENTS IN CIVILIZATION I'VE SEEN SO FAR, HOT DOGS FROM A CART MIGHT BE THE VERY BEST ONE!

YOU'RE NOT FROM AROUND HERE, ARE YOU?
NOT ORIGINALLY, NO.
BUT I'M STARTING TO LIKE IT.

LET ME GUESS. YOU'RE OFF TO FIND A PHONE BOOTH TO CHANGE IN.

NO. . . I'M OFF TO SEE THE WIZARD.

GOOD-BYE.

ZZT!
ZZT!

ZZZT
ZZT!
SSKKT

ZZCRACK!

ZZT!
ZZT!
ZEEEEEEE

I ALWAYS FORGET HOW DANGEROUS TIME TRAVEL IS.
WHIZZ!
ZZT!
ZZT!

HOW ARE YOU DOING BACK THERE, BILLY?

AAH! WHERE AM I?
JUST RELAX AND HOLD ON. WE'RE INSIDE THE LIGHT.

WHERE--?
IT'S OUR **POWER OF ZEUS!** WE'RE TRAVELING BETWEEN THE ATOMS TO GO BACK IN TIME TO THE **BIG BANG** ITSELF!

THE BIG BANG IS THE EXPLOSION THAT STARTED THE UNIVERSE, AND AS WE GO BACK IN TIME, EVERYTHING AROUND US WILL SHRINK DOWN TO A **SINGLE POINT!**
BUT DON'T WORRY --

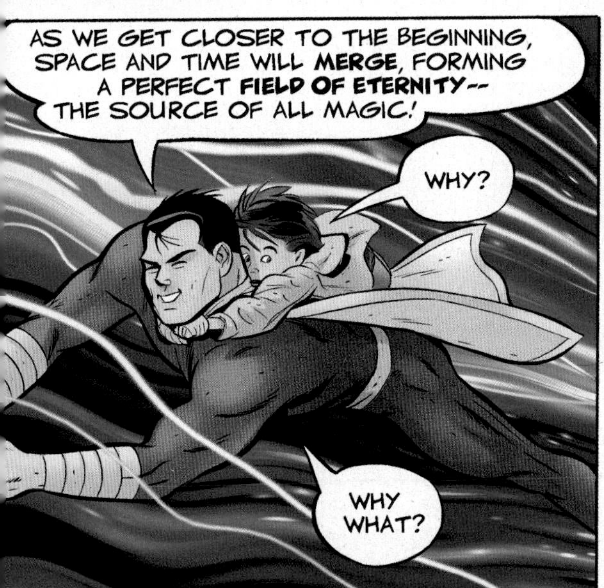
AS WE GET CLOSER TO THE BEGINNING, SPACE AND TIME WILL **MERGE**, FORMING A PERFECT **FIELD OF ETERNITY**-- THE SOURCE OF ALL MAGIC!
WHY?
WHY WHAT?

WHY ARE WE GOING TO THE **BIG BANG?!**
BECAUSE THAT'S WHERE THE WIZARD LIVES!

THERE IT IS, BILLY. THE **ROCK OF ETERNITY.**

UP ON THE PEAK IS THE **MOMENT OF CREATION.** BEAUTIFUL, ISN'T IT?
WHOA.

WHAT WOULD HAPPEN IF WE KEPT GOING BACK IN TIME? WHAT'S PAST THE PEAK?

PAST THE MOMENT OF CREATION? NOTHING!
HOW CAN THERE BE NOTHING? THERE MUST BE SOMETHING.

THERE MAY HAVE BEEN A UNIVERSE BEFORE OURS, BUT IT'S GONE NOW. IT DOES NOT EXIST TO US.
COOL! LET'S GO LOOK!

NO. WE CAN NEVER GO TO THE TOP OF THE MOUNTAIN. IT IS FORBIDDEN.
SAYS WHO?
SAYS THE WIZARD.

OH, YEAH, HIM.
YES. . .NOW LET'S GO. HE'S WAITING FOR US.

TAKE YOUR SHOES OFF. THIS IS A SACRED PLACE.

REMEMBER THESE GUYS?
RIDE ENVY GREED HATRED SELFISH

WHY ARE THEIR EYES CLOSED? ARE THEY ASLEEP?
YOU'LL FIND OUT.
INJUS

FOOM!

STAND HERE.
ZZT
CRACKLE

BOOM!
ZZT!
ZZT!

MASTER, CAN YOU HEAR US?

AH, YES. MY BOYS HAVE COME TO SEE ME.
HOW ARE YOU, BILLY BATSON?

I'VE HAD A PRETTY CRAZY WEEK, SIR.
I DON'T DOUBT IT.

MASTER, WE ARE HERE BECAUSE OF BILLY'S IVING CONDITIONS. HE SLEEPS IN A CONDEMNED UILDING. HE HAS NO FRIENDS HIS OWN AGE, AND HE HAS NO FAMILY TO TAKE CARE OF HIM.
WAIT A MINUTE!

I CAN TAKE CARE OF MYSELF! I DON'T NEED A FAMILY. I TOLD THE LADY FROM THE SHELTER I DON'T WANT A FAMILY!
BILLY--

MY MOM AND DAD DIED AND LEFT ME ALONE, BUT I **FIGURED OUT HOW TO LIVE!** I DON'T NEED **ANYONE!**
BILLY, I CHOSE YOU TO BE MY REPLACEMENT **BECAUSE** YOU ARE RESPONSIBLE AND SELF-RELIANT. . .

BUT EVERYONE NEEDS SOMEONE.
HOLD STILL A MOMENT.

HMM. YES . . .

OH! WELL! LOOK AT **THAT!**

YOU HAVE A BABY **SISTER!**

HE LOOKS SURPRISED.
HE **IS** SURPRISED. **I'M** SURPRISED.
I WONDER WHERE SHE IS?

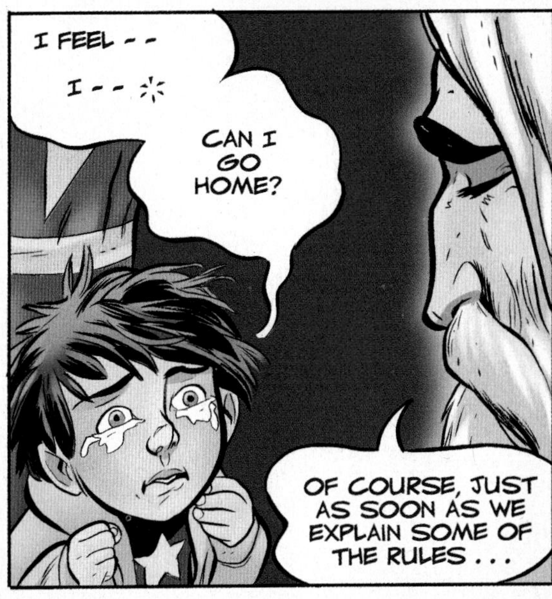
I FEEL - -
I - -
CAN I GO HOME?
OF COURSE, JUST AS SOON AS WE EXPLAIN SOME OF THE RULES . . .

WHAT RULES? I JUST HAVE TO SAY **SHAZ** - -
NO!! DON'T SAY IT, BILLY! MAGIC IS **UN-PREDICTABLE** HERE!
THIS IS **VERY IMPORTANT!** THE RULES OF THE **ORDINARY** WORLD DO NOT APPLY IN ETERNITY.

WHY?
BECAUSE **TIME** AND **SPACE** ARE SMASHED TOGETHER HERE - - LIKE IN A **BLACK HOLE!**
I'M YOUR **FUTURE SELF!**
CALLING UPON THE MAGIC **HERE** COULD CAUSE A TERRIBLE PARADOX!

PRIDE EN
PERHAPS YOU'D LIKE TO WAIT OUTSIDE FOR CAPTAIN MARVEL.

HE'S VERY YOUNG.
AND YET YOU AND HE ARE ONE. **TOGETHER** YOU WILL SOLVE YOUR PROBLEMS.
PRIDE

I'LL DO MY BEST TO WATCH OVER HIM, MASTER, BUT I MUST CONFESS THERE ARE **BLANK SPOTS** IN MY MEMORY.
OH, DEAR . . .

NO NEED FOR CONCERN, THE MEMORIES WILL RETURN. JUST MORE **SLOWLY** THAN I WOULD LIKE . . .
NO, NO. LOOK AT THE **STATUES!**

THREE - - NO, **FOUR** OF THE STATUES HAVE OPENED THEIR **EYES!**
PRIDE.
GREED, SELFISHNESS, AND **HATRED!**
INJUSTICE IS OPENING ITS EYES! THAT MAKES **FIVE!**
PRIDE
ENVY
EED

FIVE STATUES AT ONCE! AND I DO NOT LIKE THIS CONFIGURATION AT ALL. THIS COULD BE A LARGE-SCALE EVENT!
TAKE THE BOY AND HURRY BACK TO **EARTH!**
ENVY
HAT

BILLY!
WHERE IS HE?

HIS SHOES ARE GONE. BUT THERE'S NOWHERE TO GO EXCEPT THE TOP OF THE **MOUNTAIN** - -
HOLY MOLEY!

YOU DID TELL HIM THAT THE TOP OF THE MOUNTAIN WAS FORBIDDEN. . . ?
YES, I TOLD HIM!

BILLY!
GET HIM DOWN! **QUICKLY!!**

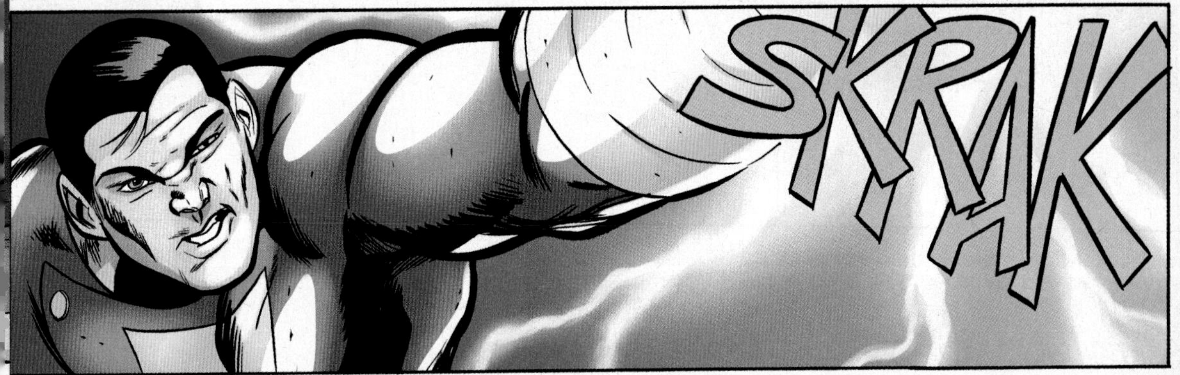
SKRAK

OH, YEAH, YOU'RE GONNA MEET **MR. MIND** . . .
IN FACT, I GOT A FEELIN' HE'S **LOOKIN'** FOR **YOU**.
POLICE

THE MONSTER SOCIETY OF EVIL

CHAPTER 2:
NZIB GZPVH GSV XZPV!*

*THE MONSTER SOCIETY CODE

A	B	C	D	E	F	G	H	I	J	K	L	M	N	O	P	Q	R	S	T	U	V	W	X	Y	Z
Z	Y	X	W	V	U	T	S	R	Q	P	O	N	M	L	K	J	I	H	G	F	E	D	C	B	A

MY MOTHER AND FATHER DIED, BUT I FIGURED OUT HOW TO LIVE! I DON'T NEED ANYONE!
EVERYONE NEEDS SOMEONE, BILLY BATSON. HOLD STILL.
HMM . . . OH! WELL! LOOK AT THAT!
YOU HAVE A BABY SISTER!
BUT WHERE IS SHE?
CLICK!
- - LOOKS LIKE ANOTHER COLD DAY IN THE CITY.

MMMM...
SQUINCH
SQUINCH
THAT'S RIGHT, HELEN. ANOTHER BLAST OF FREEZING AIR IS MOVING IN FROM THE NORTH -- STAY **INDOORS** IF YOU CAN . . .

IT **IS** COLD. I'D BETTER GO CHECK ON OL' **TALKY**.
MEANWHILE, POLICE ARE STILL ON THE SCENE OF LAST NIGHT'S **MONSTER SIGHTINGS** . . .

MULTIPLE REPORTS CAME IN CLAIMING **LARGE BANDS** OF **ALLIGATOR** PEOPLE WERE ROAMING THE STREETS.

WHEN POLICE RESPONDED, MOST OF THE CREATURES DISAPPEARED INTO THE **PARK** WHERE POLICE DISCOVERED TWO GIGANTIC **CROP CIRCLES** IN THE SHAPE OF FOOTPRINTS.
POLICE

AUTHORITIES STILL DO NOT KNOW WHO IS RESPONSIBLE FOR THE FOOTPRINTS, BUT THERE IS SPECULATION THE CROP CIRCLES AND THE ALLIGATOR MONSTERS MAY BE CONNECTED.

WITNESSES ALSO SAW A LARGE MAN IN RED CIRCUS TIGHTS ROUNDING UP MANY OF THE MONSTERS. POLICE SAY THEY WANT TO QUESTION HIM.

CAPTAIN MARVEL! OH . . . HE TOLD ME NOT TO CLIMB THE ROCK OF ETERNITY, BUT I DID ANYWAY! AND NOW THE POLICE ARE LOOKING FOR HIM!

THERE ARE SOME WHO FEAR THE STRANGE CROP CIRCLES MAY THREATEN OUR NATIONAL SECURITY. ONE WHO THINKS SO IS OUR NEW ATTORNEY GENERAL . . .

. . . DR. SIVANA.
THE DOCTOR PROMISES HIS NEWLY FORMED DEPARTMENT OF TECHNOLOGY AND HEARTLAND SECURITY WILL GET TO THE BOTTOM OF THE MONSTER PHENOMENON.

ATTORNEY GENERAL SIVANA IS SCHEDULED TO MAKE A STATEMENT ON THE COURTHOUSE STEPS IN JUST A FEW MINUTES. WE'LL BRING YOU THE DOCTOR'S SPEECH **LIVE** - - AFTER THIS BREAK!
SNN

COME ONE, COME ALL! THE CIRCUS IS IN TOWN!!
LA-TA-TOTTY-TOTTY-TOT-TAH TAH DAH

HMM . . . **THAT'S** WHAT I SHOULD DO. **JOIN THE CIRCUS!** SAY THE MAGIC WORD AND WATCH THE FREAK PICK UP AN **ELEPHANT**.
AND DON'T MISS THE WORLD'S **GREATEST** COLLECTION OF **CLAWS, JAWS AND MAN-EATING TEETH!**

IN A SPECIAL MATINEE TODAY YOU CAN SEE THE WORLD'S MOST FAMOUS **DEATH-DEFYING ACT** - - *THE MONSTER SOCIETY OF EVIL!*
GROWL! ROAR!

MONSTER SOCIETY OF **EVIL**, HM?
MAYBE I **WILL** GO DOWN THERE. . .
CLICK

EVEN IF THERE'S NO CONNECTION TO THE **ALLIGATOR PEOPLE**, I CAN AT LEAST TRY TO GET A JOB CLEANING UP AFTER THE ANIMALS.

CIRCUS LIFE, HERE I COME!
HONK HONK!

CIRCUS
CIRCUS
MATINEE TODAY!
SNN

SAY, THERE'S THAT PRETTY NEWSWOMAN!

WOW.
OH, LITTLE BOY!

ME?
YES. . .

. . . YOU'RE STANDING ON MY MICROPHONE WIRE.

OH! I DIDN'T - -
GET AWAY, YOU BRAT!
WE'RE ABOUT TO GO ON THE AIR!

BEAT IT, KID. WE DON'T NEED ANY HELP HERE.
LADIES AND GENTLEMEN. . .

. . . ATTORNEY GENERAL SIVANA WILL NOW MAKE A BRIEF STATEMENT. DR. SIVANA.

OH, I'M SORRY, SIR. DO YOU NEED HELP?
GET ME A BOX TO STAND ON, YOU FOOL!

HERE, LET ME ADJUST THE MICRO-PHONES - -
RR-SQUEENK!
I CAN DO IT MYSELF!

WHEEE--
SQUEEEE---
IS THIS THING ON?
GOOD.
HELLO.

LAST NIGHT AT APPROXIMATELY NINE P.M. A SET OF FOOTPRINTS AN ACRE WIDE APPEARED IN OUR PARK. YOUR GOVERNMENT IS WORKING AROUND THE CLOCK TO FIND THOSE RESPONSIBLE. . .

. . .THE FOOTPRINTS MAY BE WARNING US OF A TERRORIST PLOT, OR THEY MAY BE A HOAX, BUT WE HAVE THE TECHNOLOGY TO FIND WHOEVER CAUSED THIS!
WHIZ

YOU HAVE MY PERSONAL ASSURANCE THAT THE DEPARTMENT OF TECHNOLOGY AND HEARTLAND SECURITY WILL GO THROUGH THE CREDIT ACCOUNTS OF EVERY CITIZEN UNTIL WE FIND SOMETHING SUSPICIOUS!

AND WHEN WE DO, WE'LL LOCK THE EVILDOERS UP, AND THROW AWAY THE KEY!!

REMEMBER, THE TERRORISTS WIN IF WE CHANGE OUR LIFESTYLES, SO GO IMMEDIATELY TO YOUR LOCAL MALL AND SPEND, SPEND, SPEND!
KEEP OUR ECONOMY STRONG!!
YAY!
CLAP! CLAP
SNN
I'LL NEVER UNDER-STAND GROWN-UPS.

HEY, WHAT'S THIS?
ANTS?

WHOA. NO WAY! THIS MUST BE THE BIGGEST ANT WAR EVER!
SNN

WAIT A MINUTE . . . IT CAN'T BE A WAR, ALL THE ANTS ARE GOING IN THE SAME DIRECTION!
BUT TO WHERE?

WHAM!
CRUNCH! GRIND!

HEY! CUT IT OUT!

WHOOPS.
WHERE'S MY MONEY, BILLY?

IT'S NOT YOURS, LAGREEN! IT'S MINE, I EARNED IT!

IF YOU LIVE ON MY STREET, YOU PAY ME MY PIECE - - OR ELSE I TAKE IT ALL.
LET'S GET HIM AWAY FROM THIS CROWD . . .

YEAH, RIGHT.
HEY!
SNN

WHATCHA DOIN', BILLY BOY?
CHING CHING

GONNA RUN AWAY AND JOIN THE CIRCUS? HA! HA! GOOD!
THAT'S WHERE YOU BELONG - - WITH THE OTHER FREAKS!

BITE ME, LAGREEN.

GET BACK HERE!
SLIP!

CHINK!

LADIES & GENTLEMEN!

THE ACT YOU'VE WAITED TO SEE...

...THE GREAT CARLINI & HIS WORLD FAMOUS MONSTER SOCIETY OF EVIL!!

HOORAY!
THANK YOU! THANK YOU! I, THE GREAT CARLINI, HAVE TAMED THE MOST DANGEROUS MAN-EATING MONSTERS ON EARTH!!
DO NOT BE AFRAID...

EEE!
I AM ABOUT TO OPEN THE CAGES!

GOT YOU NOW, BILLY BATSON!

EEEEE!
SOMETHING IS WRONG!

THE MONSTERS HAVE EATEN THE GREAT CARLINI!
AAH!

IT'S TERRIBLE!
IT'S THE ALLIGATOR MONSTERS!

EVERYONE STAY CALM! THERE'S NO NEED FOR EVERYONE TO GET HURT...
NO, INDEED...

...ALL WE WANT...

--IS THE CHILDREN!

HA! HA! HA! TENDER, JUICY CHILDREN!
NO!

OH, MY GOSH...

THAT'S MY SISTER!

SHAZAM!

BOOM!

WHAT WAS THAT?

SPLAT!

HISSSS SSSSS
I WANT THE REST OF THE CHILDREN NOW.

DID YOU SEE WHAT JUST HAPPENED TO BATSON?
WHO CARES? LET'S GET OUT OF HERE!

WE OUTNUMBER YOU, HUMAN.
...
EXCUSE ME ...

!
BROTHER TIGER!
IS THIS A PRIVATE FIGHT, OR CAN ANYONE JOIN?

THE TIGER IS LOOSE! RUN!
THE CHILDREN ARE DOOMED!

STAY UP HERE FOR A MOMENT.

OUT OF MY WAY, TIGER.

RELAX, CAPTAIN. I'M ON YOUR SIDE.

WHAT?
WHAT WILL OUR GREAT LEADER, MR. MIND, SAY?!

I DON'T WORK FOR MR. MIND.

AAIEE!
ROAR!
RUN! WE ARE BETRAYED!

NO! YOU'LL NEVER GET THESE KIDS BACK--
WOMP!

RUN FOR THE EXIT!
MOMMY!
HISSSS!!

ROAR!
WE'VE LOST! QUICK! EAT THE CHILDREN!

HELP THEM!

CRUNCH
OH, NO YOU DON'T.

RUN.

IN YOU GO!

NOW WHERE'D THAT **TIGER** GET TO?
CLANG!

GONE!

AND SO IS BILLY'S LITTLE SISTER.

OFFICER! WARN YOUR MEN! THERE'S A TIGER ON THE LOOSE!
FORGET THE TIGER - -

WE HAVE A MUCH **BIGGER** PROBLEM! **LOOK!**

HOLY MOLEY!

WHAT IS IT?
HOW WOULD I KNOW? IT JUST APPEARED THERE!
POLICE

I GOTTA CALL THIS IN TO HEARTLAND SECURITY - - THAT THING IS STANDING IN THOSE FOOTPRINTS!
IN THE FOOTPRINTS - - !?

I HAVE TO GET BILLY'S SISTER TO SAFETY!

EXCUSE ME, HAVE YOU SEEN A LITTLE GIRL HOLDING A DOLL? SHE HAS A PINK COAT- -

ATTENTION, CAPTAIN MARVEL...

I AM MR. MIND....

...I COME TO YOUR WORLD TO REMOVE ALL TRACE OF HUMAN CIVILIZATION...

ALL THE OTHER CREATURES OF EARTH WILL JOIN WITH ME...AND REJOICE!

HOW DO YOU KNOW MY NAME?

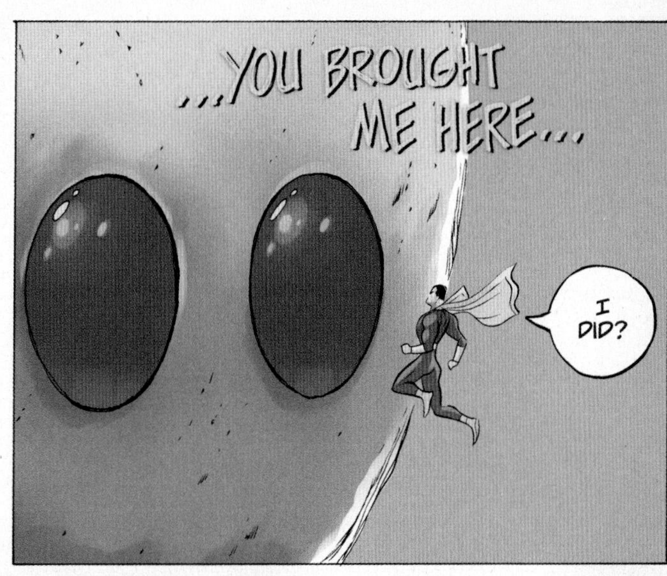
...YOU BROUGHT ME HERE...
I DID?

...I COME FROM BEYOND CREATION...

BEYOND THE ROCK OF ETERNITY.

WE SHALL MAKE OF YOUR WORLD A GLORIOUS SOCIETY...
A SOCIETY OF CREATURES YOU WOULD CALL MONSTERS...
!

YOU'LL HAVE TO GO THROUGH ME FIRST.

TWO COMPANIONS WILL JOIN ME... THEN THE DESTRUCTION OF YOUR RACE WILL BEGIN...

BAM
KRACK

KRAK!
POW!
POW!
POW!
BAM!

NOT EVEN A MARK . . . THOSE BLOWS WOULD KNOCK THE TOP OFF A **MOUNTAIN.**

THIS BEING IS MORE POWERFUL THAN I GUESSED.

I HATE TO **ADMIT** IT- - I HAVE NO CHOICE BUT TO WAIT FOR **MR. MIND'S** NEXT MESSAGE!

NOT CROS
HONK! HONK!
MAKE WAY! LET US THROUGH!

I'M SORRY, SIR. THE POLICE AREN'T LETTING ANYONE GET CLOSER TO THE CREATURE.
I'M THE ATTORNEY GENERAL! I CAN DO ANYTHING I WANT!

WAIT--! STOP THE CAR!

POLICE

HMMM.

SHE'S JUST A LITTLE GIRL . . .
. . . HOW FAR COULD SHE HAVE GONE?

THERE SHE IS - - BY THE RIVERFRONT!

HOORAY! YOU FOUND ME! I KNEW YOU WOULD!

MY NAME IS MARY! WHAT'S YOURS?

I'M CAPTAIN MARVEL - -
YOU'RE MY HERO, MR. MARVEL!
SMACK! SMACK!
I LOVE YOU!

MARY, LISTEN! I HAVE GOOD NEWS! I'M YOUR BROTHER!

WHAT?

WELL, SORT OF . . .
I DON'T HAVE A BROTHER.

WAIT . . .
MR. TAWNY!
TROUBLE, MARY? THE GOOD CAPTAIN WON'T HURT YOU.

!
YOU AGAIN! GET BEHIND ME, MARY!
NO! DON'T FIGHT!

NOT TO WORRY, DEAR. CAPTAIN MARVEL AND I ARE OLD FRIENDS, ISN'T THAT RIGHT, BILLY?

WHAT'S GOING ON HERE?
DON'T YOU RECOGNIZE YOUR OLD NEIGHBOR? YOU USED TO RUN ERRANDS INTO THE CITY FOR ME . . .

IT'S ME, TALKY TAWNY! I ADMIT I LOOK A LITTLE DIFFERENT, BUT THE FUR HELPS KEEP MY OLD HIPS WARM.

TALKY?! IT'S YOU? BUT HOW?! YOU WERE A MAN!
I'M AN IFRIT, BOY! A WANDERING SPIRIT THAT CHANGES FROM HUMAN TO ANIMAL!
APPARENTLY YOUR MEMORY HASN'T FULLY RETURNED.

YOU SEE, I WORK FOR THE WIZARD, TOO! AND RIGHT NOW, MY JOB IS TO MAKE SURE YOU ARE ADJUSTING TO YOUR NEW LIFE!
SIT! SIT!

MY NEW LIFE . . . BUT WHY DID YOU TURN YOURSELF INTO A TIGER?
I WAS A TIGER FIRST, BUT I CAN'T WALK AROUND THE CITY AS A TIGER, CAN I?

I GUESS NOT. SO, AM I AN IFRIT, AS WELL?
NO, YOU ARE A FORCE OF NATURE - - A PROTECTOR GUARDIAN. THAT MEANS YOU HAVE JOINED WITH A MORTAL WHOSE NAME IS BILLY BATSON.

SPEAKING OF WHICH, WHEN WAS THE LAST TIME YOU LET HIM OUT TO BREATHE?
OH, MY GOSH! I ALMOST FORGOT!
SHAZAM!

BOOM
NOW LISTEN TO ME, BILLY BATSON! THIS IS IMPORTANT. . .
GASP! HUFF! HUFF!

PUFF! GULP!
DO YOU REMEMBER EVERYTHING THAT HAPPENED WHILE YOU WERE CAPTAIN MARVEL? DO YOU REMEMBER THE APPEARANCE OF MR. MIND?

HUFF PUFF! EVERYTHING!
I REMEMBER EVERYTHING.
WONDERFUL. THAT IS A SIGN YOU AND THE CAPTAIN ARE A GOOD FIT!
TOGETHER YOU WILL MAKE A POWERFUL GUARDIAN!

WOW. YOU REALLY LOOKED LIKE TALKY THERE FOR A SECOND.
HEY, KID! HOW DID YOU DO THAT?
BECOME A KID?

I HAVE A MAGIC WORD - - I CAN CHANGE BACK AND FORTH!
YUK! I KISSED YOU!

OH, COME ON. IT'S NOT SO BAD KISSING YOUR BROTHER!
THAT'S EVEN WORSE! CHANGE BACK INTO CAPTAIN MARVEL AND TAKE ME FLYING!

I'M NOT A **RIDE.**
WELL, WILL YOU TAKE ME HOME AND LET ME LIVE AT YOUR HOUSE?

HUH? I DON'T HAVE A HOUSE - - OR ANY **PARENTS.** MAYBE WE SHOULD GO TO **YOUR** HOUSE.
I DON'T HAVE A HOUSE EITHER.

SURE YOU DO. LOOK HOW NICE YOUR CLOTHES ARE.
I USED TO LIVE WITH MRS. BROMFIELD, BUT I RAN AWAY.

MARY **BROMFIELD.**
NEVER CALL ME THAT! THAT'S NOT MY NAME!

SORRY! WHAT HAPPENED?
I RAN AWAY TO JOIN THE CIRCUS.

NEVER MIND. YOU'LL JUST MAKE FUN OF ME.

MRS. BROMFIELD WAS MY FOSTER MOTHER, AND SHE'S HATED ME EVER SINCE MR. BROMFIELD LEFT.

SHE SAID IT WAS MY FAULT, AND SHE WISHED I WAS DEAD.

WOW.
PLEASE LET ME STAY WITH YOU, BILLY. **PLEASE?**

VELL, I GUESS YOU'LL HAVE TO FOR A WHILE.
I SHOULD WARN YOU, THOUGH, IT ISN'T A VERY NICE PLACE.
OH, THANK YOU!

IT'S IN AN ABANDONED BUILDING UNDER THE EAST BRIDGE . . . BOY, I HOPE THIS IS THE RIGHT THING TO DO.

I MEAN, IT'S ONE THING FOR ME TO BE ON THE STREET, BUT MY LITTLE SISTER CAN'T LIVE LIKE THAT!
BILLY?

WHAT?
DO YOU THINK RUNNING AWAY TO JOIN THE CIRCUS WAS A STUPID IDEA?

NAW. IT WAS A COOL IDEA.

BILLY. . .

DO YOU KNOW WHAT THE HOUR IS?

NO, I DON'T HAVE A WATCH.

IT IS THE HOUR OF TWO LIGHTS.

IN TWILIGHT, DAY HAS NOT ENDED AND NIGHT HAS NOT STARTED. THINGS ARE UNSETTLED. . .

. . . SPIRITS ARE RESTLESS.

WHAT DOES THAT MEAN?
IT MEANS IF SOMETHING IS GOING TO HAPPEN, IT IS GOING TO HAPPEN NOW.

uh, oh!
LOOK!

THE FIRST COMPANION! MR. MIND'S THREAT IS COMING TRUE! THERE'S ONLY ONE MORE MONSTER TO GO!
GO ON, BILLY! SAY IT. TURN INTO CAPTAIN MARVEL!

BUT CAPTAIN MARVEL WASN'T ABLE TO DO ANYTHING ABOUT THE **FIRST** MONSTER - - WHAT CAN HE DO AGAINST **TWO**?

CAPTAIN MARVEL MUST NEVER BE DAUNTED BY THE ODDS - - YOU ARE THE GUARDIAN OF ALL THOSE WHO CANNOT DEFEND THEMSELVES.

UT I'M JUST LITTLE KID.
YOU ARE **CAPTAIN MARVEL.**
YAY!

WHAT'S WRONG WITH YOU? I'VE KNOWN YOU FOR A LONG TIME, AND I'VE NEVER SEEN YOU SCARED OF **ANYTHING!**

I HAVE A CONFESSION TO MAKE. **MR. MIND** AND HIS MONSTER SOCIETY ARE HERE BECAUSE OF ME.

YOU KNOW THOSE **FOOTPRINTS** MR. MIND IS STANDING IN?
I MADE THOSE FOOTPRINTS ON TOP OF **THE ROCK OF ETERNITY** - - I WANTED TO SEE IF THERE WAS ANOTHER **UNIVERSE** BEFORE OURS . . .

THE WIZARD **TOLD** ME THE TOP OF THE MOUNTAIN WAS FORBIDDEN, BUT, WELL . . .
. . . I KINDA BLANKED OUT AND DIDN'T SEE MUCH.

BUT **I** MADE THOSE FOOTPRINTS AND BROUGHT **MR. MIND** HERE! I MADE THIS WHOLE **MESS!**
ALL THE MORE REASON FOR YOU TO CLEAN IT UP.

BUT WHAT IF I SCREW UP AGAIN? I'LL MAKE THINGS **WORSE!**

NO MORE SCREW-UPS. MAKE THE WIZARD **PROUD** OF YOU, OKAY?
BILLY?

OKAY!
WHAT ARE YOU WAITING FOR? **SAY THE MAGIC WORD!**

SHAZAM!

KRAK

BOOM!

CRASH!
HONK HONK HONK HONK

WHERE'S MARY?
SHE WAS HIT BY YOUR **LIGHTNING!**

CRACKLE!
ZZT!

NO!

MARY!

PCHUNK!

RRRR

RRRRRRK

KRUNK
PLEASE DON'T GET MAD AT ME . . .

MARY - - ARE YOU HURT?

LOOK. I HAVE A COSTUME . . .

LIKE **YOURS.**

I THINK YOU SHOULD SIT DOWN - - YOU PROBABLY SHOULDN'T **MOVE** UNTIL WE MAKE SURE YOU'RE ALL RIGHT.
I WONDER . . .

WHOA.

BAM
CRASH
POW!

YOU KNOW WHAT I THINK?
WHAT?

I THINK THESE GUYS ARE ROBOTS . . .
!

. . . AND MR. MIND IS EITHER INSIDE ONE OF THEM, OR CONTROLLING THEM FROM SOMEWHERE ELSE.
HMM.

C'MON OUT, MR. MIND! WHAT'RE YOU WAITING FOR?

WHAT'S THE MATTER?! SCARED?
I DON'T THINK HE'S SCARED. I THINK HE'S WAITING FOR THE LAST MONSTER TO ARRIVE.

ONCE THE THIRD MONSTER APPEARS, MR. MIND SAID HE WAS GOING TO WIPE OUT HUMAN CIVILIZATION.
WHY?

I DON'T KNOW YET, BUT IF YOU'RE RIGHT ABOUT THESE GUYS BEING ROBOTS -- MAYBE WE CAN FIGURE OUT WHAT MAKES THEM TICK AND DISABLE THEM.
WAIT A MINUTE ...

DID YOU FEEL THAT? A REALLY SPOOKY CHILL RUNNING UP AND DOWN YOUR BACK --?

BUP BUP BUP BUP
ATTENTION, CAPTAIN MARVEL! THIS IS THE DEPARTMENT of HEARTLAND SECURITY!
WE ORDER YOU TO LAND AND SURRENDER!
D-THS

TAKE IT EASY- -
WE'RE ON YOUR SIDE!

TATTA! TA-TTA! TATTA

WATCH OUT, MARY!
SPOW!
SPIING!
TAT! TAT!
POW! POW!
TAT! TATTA TATTA TATTA

WHY ARE THEY SHOOTING AT US?
THEY MUST THINK WE'RE IN LEAGUE WITH THE MONSTERS - - BUT THEY DIDN'T EVEN **TRY** TO FIND OUT.
HALT!

HEY! LET ME GO! I WANNA FIND OUT IF I'M BULLETPROOF LIKE YOU!
NO!
NOW HOLD TIGHT. I'M GOING TO LOSE THEM.

WHOA!
SHHHHHH''''''

SON OF A - - DID YOU SEE THAT?!
HE'S GONE! TOOK OFF LIKE A ROCKET.
ANYONE GOT A FIX?

ZZT - - NEGATIVE.
SUSPECT HAS FLED THE SCENE.
BETTER RADIO THE BOSS AND TELL HIM WE LOST THEM.

SHAZAM!
SHAZAM!

BUHBOOM!

WHERE ARE WE, BILLY?
THIS IS WHERE I LIVE. HOLD ON I'VE RIGGED UP A LIGHT OVER HERE.

BEFORE I TURN IT ON THOUGH, I HAVE TO ASK, ARE YOU AFRAID OF BUGS?
YES!
YOU MIGHT WANT TO BRACE YOURSELF.

CLICK!
HEY! WHERE'RE THE ROACHES?

CAN I OPEN MY EYES YET?
I DON'T GET IT. USUALLY WHEN I TURN THE LIGHT ON, MILLIONS OF ROACHES SCATTER . . .

NOW THERE ISN'T A SINGLE ONE!
IS THAT BLANKET YOUR BED?

YEAH. I'M SORRY, MARY. I TOLD YOU THIS PLACE WASN'T VERY NICE. MAYBE I SHOULD TAKE YOU DOWN TO THE SHELTER.
OH, LOOK! A TV!

WHERE DID ALL THE **BUGS** GO? HELEN FIDELITY HAS THIS REPORT - -
WHERE'S THE **CARTOON CHANNEL?**

WAIT!
YES, JUNE, IT SEEMS THE BUGS HAVE **BUGGED OUT!**
STRANGE AS IT SOUNDS, ALL THE INSECTS IN THE CITY HAVE **DISAPPEARED!**
WE VISITED THE OWNER OF **CITY EXTERMINATORS** TO FIND OUT WHAT'S GOING ON.

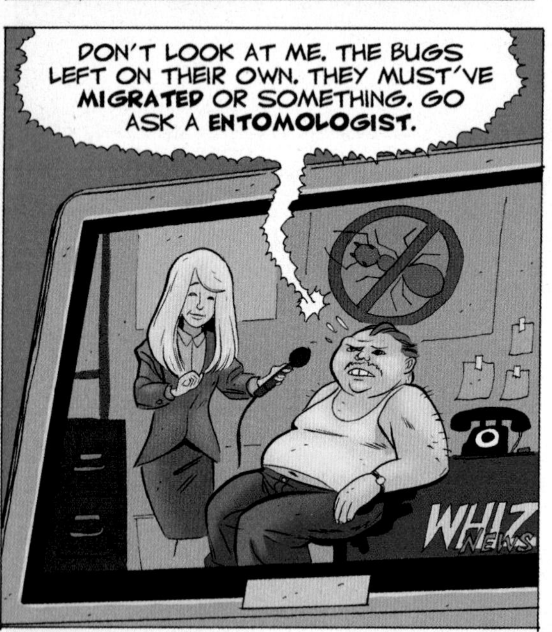
DON'T LOOK AT ME. THE BUGS LEFT ON THEIR OWN. THEY MUST'VE **MIGRATED** OR SOMETHING. GO ASK A **ENTOMOLOGIST.**
WHIZ NEWS

SO IT'S **TRUE!** ALL THE BUGS ARE GONE AND EVERYONE IS **CELEBRATING!**
I'M NOT.
WELL, EVERYONE BUT **YOU.** YOU'RE OUT OF A **JOB!** ISN'T THIS A **FABULOUS DAY?!**
I SAW THAT HUGE SWARM OF **ANTS** MARCHING TOWARD THE PARK TODAY. THAT **CAN'T** BE A COINCIDENCE.

HEY!
SOUNDS LIKE SOMEONE IS AT THE DOOR.
WHAT? **MARY - -**
NO!

BAM
EEE!

COVER THEIR MOUTHS SO THEY CAN'T SAY THEIR MAGIC WORDS.

YOU CAN COME IN NOW, BOYS.
IS THIS THEM?

YEAH, THAT'S THEM.
THANK YOU. YOU HAVE BEEN VERY HELPFUL TO YOUR GOVERNMENT. NOW WAIT IN THE HALL.

WELL, WELL, WELL. . . WE KNOW A LITTLE SECRET ABOUT **YOU**, DON'T WE?

TIE THEIR HANDS AND PUT TAPE OVER THEIR MOUTHS.
ZZZP

DO YOU SEE THIS PAD AND PENCIL, BILLY BATSON? IF YOU WANT TO ANSWER ANY OF MY QUESTIONS. . .

. . . JUST WRITE IT DOWN **HERE.**

NOW, **WHY** WOULD **THE ATTORNEY GENERAL OF THE UNITED STATES** BE STANDING IN YOUR FILTHY ROOM WHILE TWO **ALIEN MONSTERS ARE THREATENING THE AMERICAN PUBLIC?**

BECAUSE THE ENTIRE CITY WITNESSED A FLYING MAN IN RED TIGHTS TALKING TO THE MONSTERS -- AND I KNOW THAT THIS FLYING CAPTAIN MARVEL IS ACTUALLY A BAD LITTLE BOY!

ARE YOU PLOTTING WITH THE ALIENS TO ATTACK OUR COUNTRY? ARE YOU?!
SCRIBBLE! SCRIBBLE!

NO. We are trying to stop them.

INTERESTING.

I HEREBY ORDER YOU TO STOP INTERACTING WITH THE CREATURES. YOU HAVE NO AUTHORITY TO ACT ON BEHALF OF THE U.S. GOVERNMENT.

but Captain Marvel can help!

HOW DARE YOU QUESTION MY ORDERS?! YOU ARE JUST A LITTLE BOY!

THE GOVERNMENT WILL DECIDE HOW BEST TO HANDLE THIS MATTER -- NOT YOU...

...OR YOUR FRIEND "CAPTAIN MARVEL"
...THAT BIG RED CHEESE!
SCRIBBLE!

MM!
WHAT'S THIS, LITTLE GIRL? THE ALIEN CREATURES ARE REALLY GIANT ROBOTS?

ALL THE MORE REASON TO KEEP THEM AROUND A WHILE LONGER.

ROBOTS ARE JUST MACHINES - - TOOLS FOR POWERFUL MEN.
TOOLS OF WAR.

AND WAR . . .
. . . IS PROFITABLE.

TAKE THE GIRL AND MEET ME AT THE RENDEZVOUS POINT.
BILLY IS COMING WITH ME.

POLICE

REMEMBER, BOYS, YOU ARE OFFICIALLY **DEPUTIZED**, SO DO EXACTLY AS I SAY.

THESE TWO ARE WITH ME. WE'RE SETTING UP SENSITIVE EQUIPMENT NEAR THE FEET OF THE MONSTERS.
YES, SIR!

I'M NOT SCARED, ARE YOU, LA GREEN?
OF COURSE NOT.

LET'S SET UP BEHIND THIS ROCK - - AWAY FROM PRYING EYES.
I DON'T WANT TO SHARE ANY PATENTS ON MY DISCOVERIES!

HAND ME THE SPEC-NOCULARS!
UNZIP!

NOW, LET'S SEE WHAT WE'RE UP AGAINST, SHALL WE?

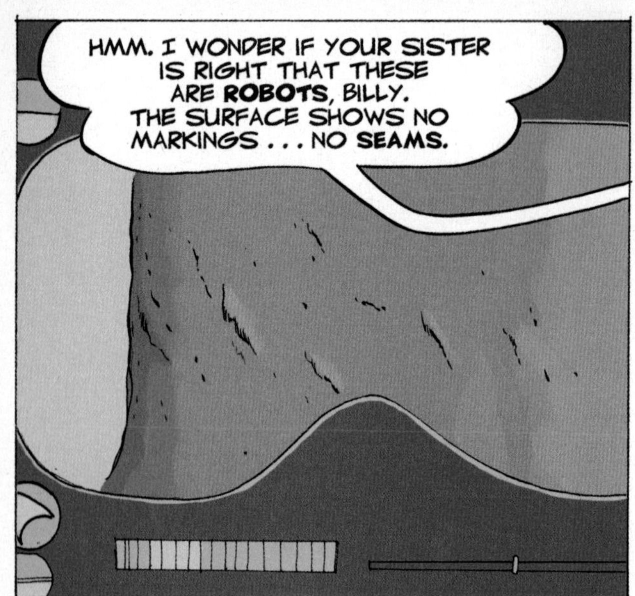
HMM. I WONDER IF YOUR SISTER IS RIGHT THAT THESE ARE ROBOTS, BILLY. THE SURFACE SHOWS NO MARKINGS . . . NO SEAMS.

IMPOSSIBLE! THE SPECTRAL READINGS ARE ZERO!
IF THE RADIATION LEVELS WEREN'T SO LOW, I'D SWEAR WE WERE LOOKING AT A BLACK HOLE!

EH? WHAT'S THIS?

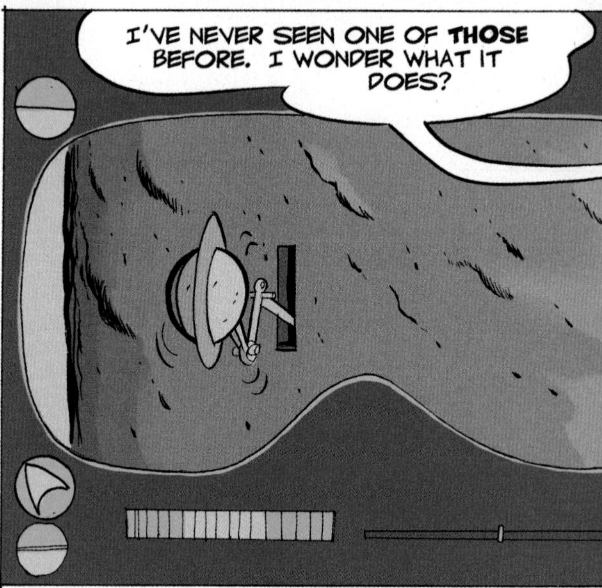
I'VE NEVER SEEN ONE OF THOSE BEFORE. I WONDER WHAT IT DOES?

ALL RIGHT, BOYS, THIS IS THE MOMENT OF TRUTH. YOUR GOVERNMENT NEEDS YOU TO RUN TOWARD THAT THING STICKING OUT OF THE MONSTER'S FEET. READY?

WHAT ARE YOU WAITING FOR?! DO YOU WANT THE **TERRORISTS** TO **WIN?!**
HELL NO!

TERRORISTS CAN'T COME INTO **MY** TOWN WITHOUT A FIGHT!
YEAH! LET'S KICK THEIR ASSES!

ZZZZZZ!

HERE WE GO - - **NOW** WE'RE GETTING SOME READINGS!
PING! PING! PING!

ZZZZZ!
EEAGH!
AA!

AAA!
WOW. DROPPED THEM IN THEIR TRACKS!
HELP!
IF I COULD SELL ONE OF **THOSE** TO THE ARMY, I'D MAKE A **FORTUNE!**

AAAH!

AMAZING. ARE THOSE GROWTHS **BACTERIAL?** MAYBE THEY'RE TUMORS . . .

ZZZZZZZZZZ
ZZZZZ!
METABOLIC GROWTH RATE IS UNBELIEVABLE. THE TRANSFORMATION SEEMS TO BE OCCURRING FROM WITHIN THEIR OWN BONES.

GROOUU...

HMM. IT'S HIGHLY UNLIKELY THEY'LL SURVIVE THIS.
PING! PING! PING! PING! PING! PING!

RRRR!

NOW SEE HERE! DON'T YOU LOOK AT ME LIKE THAT! YOU WORK FOR ME!
MM. MM!

I'M THE ATTORNEY GENERAL OF THE - -
RAAA!
MM!!

QUICK, BILLY! SAY YOUR MAGIC WORD - - WHY WON'T THIS BLASTED TAPE COME OFF?!

ACK! TOO LATE! EAT THE BOY!

MMM!

SHAZAM!

CRAK
POW!

LOOK! LOOK!

HMMMM!
ZZZZ!

NOT AT ME, YOU BIG RED CHEESE! AT THE CHANGING RAY! IT'S POINTING RIGHT AT US!!

ZZZ!
HURRY!

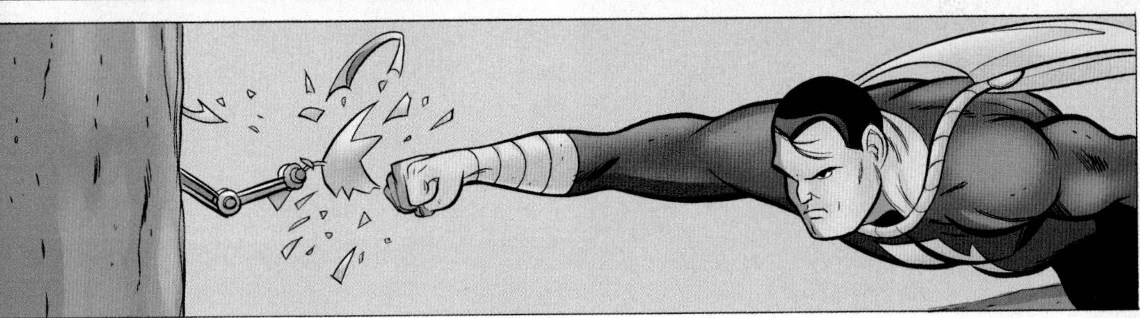

NO! DON'T BREAK IT, YOU IDIOT! IT'S WORTH MILLIONS!!
DON'T BREAK ANYTHING ELSE! REMEMBER - - I STILL HAVE YOUR SISTER!

YESSSS, CAPTAIN MARVEL. YOU SHOULD NOT HAVE BROKEN IT.
?

HOLY MOLEY!
WHERE DID ALL OF **YOU** COME FROM?
WE WERE CREATED BY **MR. MIND!**
HE AWAKENED OUR **TRUE SELVES!**
WE ARE **THE MONSTER SOCIETY**, AND YOU ARE OUR **ENEMY!**

...WITH YOUR HEAD!
CRUNCH
YEEE!
HA! HA!

CUTE.
GET HIM!
PTU!

HELP! HELP!
RRRRR

WHAT'S GOING ON IN THERE?
FIRE THE TEAR GAS!

POM!
POOM!
SSSSSS
SSSSSSS

SSSSS
THE ATTORNEY GENERAL IS IN DANGER - - YOU MEN COME WITH ME!

I CAN'T SEE A THING IN THIS TEAR GAS - -
SWISH!

GONE! THE MONSTERS VANISHED AS FAST AS THEY APPEARED!
AND IT LOOKS LIKE THEY TOOK SIVANA WITH THEM!

THIS IS THE ARMY!
WE SEE YOU, CAPTAIN MARVEL! FREEZE!!

WHERE DID HE GO? ANYBODY SEE HIM?

NEGATIVE.

HE'S GONE. SPREAD OUT AND FIND THE ATTORNEY GENERAL!
LET'S GO!

SCUFF

WHO'S THERE?
IT IS ME, BILLY. I DID NOT MEAN TO STARTLE YOU.

TALKY!
YOU'RE YOUR OLD SELF AGAIN!
ONE CANNOT WALK AROUND THE CITY AS A TIGER ALL THE TIME.

OH, TALKY! THEY TOOK MARY!
WHO DID? WHEN?

DR. SIVANA AND HIS MEN! THEY GRABBED US BOTH THIS MORNING, BUT I ESCAPED.
MY GOODNESS. WE MUST FIND HER!

I'VE TRIED! I FLEW OVER THE WHOLE CITY A DOZEN TIMES. I CAN'T FIND MARY!
HMM. I DON'T UNDERSTAND WHY THE ATTORNEY GENERAL WOULD KIDNAP TWO CHILDREN . . .

HE KNOWS OUR SECRET AND HE WANTS TO STOP US FROM GETTING RID OF MR. MIND. HE WANTS TO FIGHT THE MONSTER SOCIETY HIMSELF!
WHATEVER FOR?!

HE'S GOING TO BUILD SPECIAL WEAPONS AND SELL THEM TO THE ARMY - - SO HE CAN MAKE A FORTUNE!
WAR PROFITEERING! THAT IS IMMORAL - - AND ILLEGAL. WE CAN STOP HIM, BILLY!

HOW? WHAT CAN WE DO, TALKY?
WE'LL GO TO THE AUTHORITIES. THEY WILL HELP US.

BUT WHO CAN WE TRUST? DR. SIVANA IS THE HEAD OF THE DEPT. OF TECHNOLOGY AND HEARTLAND SECURITY. . . ALL THE AUTHORITIES WORK FOR HIM!

BESIDES, NOBODY IS GOING TO TAKE THE WORD OF A LITTLE KID OR A HOMELESS OLD MAN.

PERHAPS THEY WOULD TAKE THE WORD OF A TALKING TIGER?

I DOUBT IT.

WAIT - - ! I KNOW! WE'LL GO TO THE MEDIA!
YOU TRUST THE MEDIA?

F WE CAN EXPOSE DR. SIVANA'S SCHEME ON TV, THE POLICE AND THE FBI WILL HAVE TO HELP US . . .

AND ONCE WE CATCH SIVANA, WE'LL GET MARY BACK!
A BRILLIANT PLAN, YOUNG BILLY!

WITH MARY SAFE, AND SIVANA OUT OF THE WAY, CAPTAIN MARVEL WILL BE FREE TO DEAL WITH MR. MIND!
YES...

...AND I BELIEVE WE SHOULD HURRY. MR. MIND'S LAST COMPANION APPEARED AT TWILIGHT. THE THIRD AND FINAL COMPANION MONSTER MAY COME TONIGHT.

OKAY, HERE'S THE PLAN. YOU GO TO THE PARK AND KEEP YOUR EYES OPEN - - WATCH FOR SIVANA OR MARY. . .

I'LL GO UPTOWN TO THE TV STATION. MAYBE THAT PRETTY NEWS REPORTER WILL HELP ME.
SHE IS VERY PRETTY. I HAVE SEEN HER.

I GUESS THAT'S ALL. WE BETTER GO.
REMEMBER, IF YOU HAVE TROUBLE, YOU AND CAPTAIN MARVEL ARE **ONE** - - DON'T FORGET TO RELY ON EACH OTHER'S STRENGTHS.

WHAT ABOUT YOU? CAN YOU GET PAST THE ARMY?

I HAVE WAYS. HURRY NOW, THE HOUR OF TWO LIGHTS WILL BE HERE BEFORE WE KNOW IT.

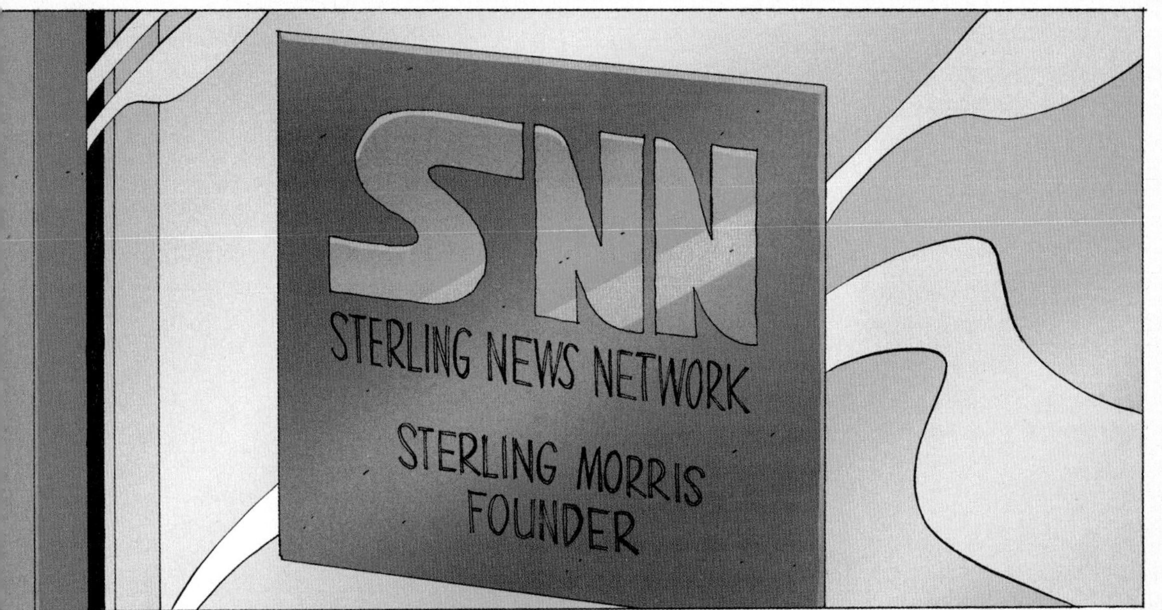
SNN
STERLING NEWS NETWORK
STERLING MORRIS
FOUNDER

STERLING MORRIS . . .
THAT'S WHO I NEED TO SEE.
TAXI

HOPE HE'S HERE.

EXCUSE ME, WHERE CAN I FIND MR. MORRIS?
CHECK AT THE DESK, KID.
SNN
SNN. HOW MAY I DIRECT YOUR CALL?

CAN I SPEAK WITH MR. MORRIS, PLEASE? I HAVE SOMETHING IMPORTANT TO TELL HIM.

DO YOU HAVE AN APPOINTMENT WITH MR. MORRIS?
UH, NO, BUT I NEED HIS HELP. MY SISTER HAS BEEN KIDNAPPED BY DR. SIVANA -- THE ATTORNEY GENERAL. I ALSO --

MR. MORRIS IS VERY BUSY, LITTLE BOY. IF YOUR SISTER IS MISSING YOU SHOULD GO TO THE POLICE.
BUT CAN'T YOU JUST TELL HIM? THERE'S MORE --

I'M SORRY. I HAVE TO GET BACK TO WORK.
JOAN, WHERE'S CHARLIE? I NEED A UNIT QUICK.
!

I'LL CHECK, HELEN. LOOKS LIKE HE'S OUT TO LUNCH.
HELEN FIDELITY!

MISS FIDELITY CAN YOU HELP ME? MY SISTER HAS BEEN **KIDNAPPED** BY DR. SIVANA --

WHERE'S YOUR MOTHER, LITTLE BOY? DOES SHE KNOW YOU'RE OUT BOTHERING GROWN UPS?

NEVER MIND.

ANYWAY, CHARLIE'S NOT BACK YET.
HOW ABOUT CHRIS? I NEED A QUICK PICK-UP IN THE PARK.

CHRIS IS AT THE PARK NOW.
PERFECT! LET HIM KNOW I'M ON MY WAY --

BOOM
!
WAS THAT THUNDER?

I THINK IT WAS MY HEART. LOOK WHAT JUST WALKED IN!

IT'S THAT MAN FROM YOUR STORY - - CAPTAIN MARVEL! THE POLICE ARE LOOKING FOR HIM.
HUBBA HUBBA!

CAN I HELP YOU?

I CAN SEE WHY THEY CALL YOU CAPTAIN MARVEL.
I HAVE INFORMATION CONCERNING THE MONSTERS AND THE WHEREABOUTS OF THE ATTORNEY GENERAL.

WHAT IS IT?
I THINK IT WOULD BE BEST IF I TOLD IT DIRECTLY TO MR. MORRIS.

YOU'RE MY STORY. YOU CAN GIVE IT TO ME.
I'LL GIVE IT TO YOU, BUT ONLY IN FRONT OF MR. MORRIS.

ALL RIGHT. WAIT OVER THERE WHILE I CALL UP TO HIS OFFICE.

SNN

DID YOU LIKE THAT, BILLY?

YES, I DID!

THAT'S FAR ENOUGH . . . THERE'S NO ONE IN HERE.
ROGER **THAT.** I DON'T WANT TO GET ANY CLOSER TO THOSE **MONSTERS** THAN I HAVE TO - -

BUDDA-BUDDA-BUDDA-BUDDA!

HO! HO! IT'S JUST A CAT!

YOU OKAY, MAN?
YEAH - - SORRY. JUST A LITTLE TENSE.

KA-CHUNK

SooooSHH!

GASP!

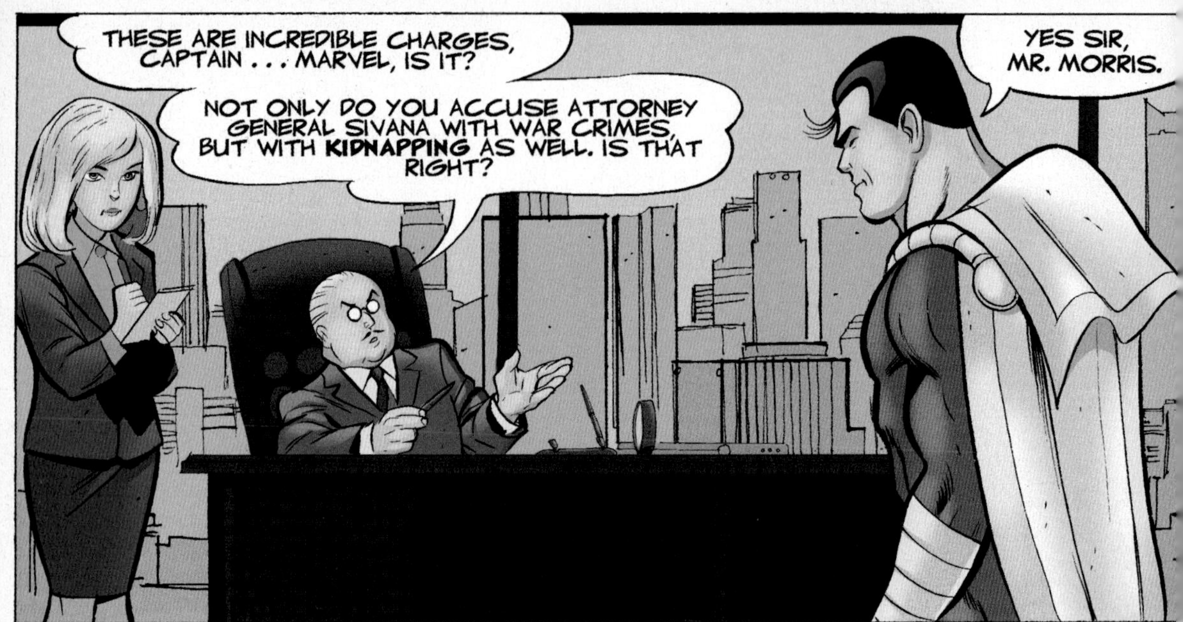
THESE ARE INCREDIBLE CHARGES, CAPTAIN . . . MARVEL, IS IT?
NOT ONLY DO YOU ACCUSE ATTORNEY GENERAL SIVANA WITH WAR CRIMES, BUT WITH **KIDNAPPING** AS WELL. IS THAT RIGHT?
YES SIR, MR. MORRIS.

AMAZING. SO TELL ME WHAT YOU WANT FROM ME.
I'M HOPING SNN WILL HELP ME EXPOSE SIVANA'S **PLOT** . . .

. . . BUT MORE IMPORTANT, I'M ASKING YOUR HELP IN FINDING THE LITTLE GIRL. PUT HER DESCRIPTION ON THE NEWS - - HAVE YOUR REPORTERS WATCH FOR SIVANA'S MEN.

OF COURSE WE WILL DO WHAT WE CAN TO FIND THE LITTLE GIRL . . .

BUT AS FAR AS **ACCUSING** ONE OF THE MOST POWERFUL MEN IN THE COUNTRY. . . I'M AFRAID WE'LL NEED A LITTLE MORE PROOF OF YOUR CLAIMS.

WHAT DO YOU SUGGEST?

WELL . . . IT WOULD HELP IF YOU COULD CATCH HIM ON CAMERA.

THE NEXT TIME YOU SPEAK WITH DR. SIVANA, OR THE NEXT TIME YOU FLY UP TO ONE OF THOSE **MONSTERS** IN THE PARK . . .

. . . TAKE **THIS** WITH YOU. IT'S A HAND-HELD SATELLITE LINK-UP CALLED GLOBAL POD.

IT'S A PROTOTYPE. THE PICTURES ARE GRAINY, AND THERE'S A SLIGHT DELAY, BUT PEOPLE ARE USED TO THAT BECAUSE OF THE WAR COVERAGE.

DO WE HAVE A DEAL?
YES.

MAY I USE YOUR WINDOW?
BE MY GUEST.

WHY DID YOU TRUST HIM, MR. MORRIS?
BECAUSE IF HE IS RIGHT, HE'LL BE DOING THIS COUNTRY A GREAT FAVOR.
AND I HAVE A BUSINESS TO RUN - - THIS COULD BE A GREAT STORY.

BUT WHAT IF CAPTAIN MARVEL IS WRONG?

THEN THE AUTHORITIES CAN USE THE GLOBAL POD TO TRACK HIS EVERY MOVE.

DO NOT CROSS

DO NOT CROSS

TALKY --

PSST! TALKY?

AAA!

SORRY. I'M STILL NOT USED TO THIS.
COME WITH ME. NEW INFORMATION HAS COME TO LIGHT.

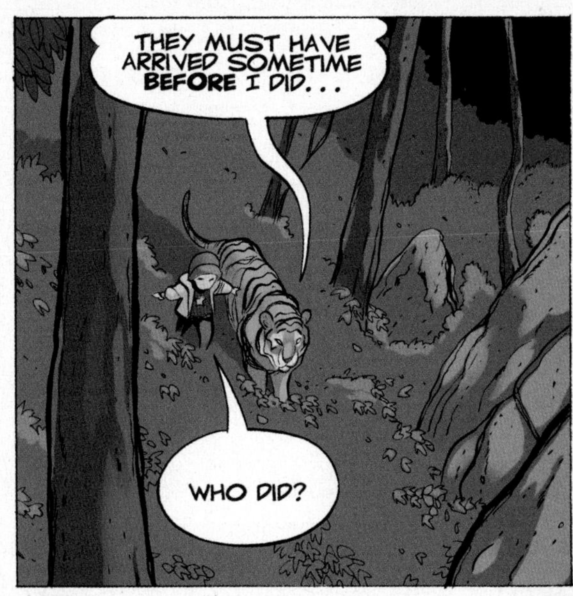
THEY MUST HAVE ARRIVED SOMETIME BEFORE I DID...
WHO DID?

THERE! BETWEEN THE MONSTER'S FEET-- STANDING WHERE THE ARMY OUTSIDE CAN'T SEE THEM.
GASP!
NO WAY. THAT'S SIVANA'S MEN...

...THE ONES WHO TOOK MARY!

YES, AND THEY'RE STANDING GUARD. I WOULDN'T BE SURPRISED IF BOTH MARY AND SIVANA WERE INSIDE.
INSIDE THE MONSTER?! WE HAVE TO GET MARY OUT OF THERE!
PATIENCE, BILLY. THINGS ARE NOT ALWAYS WHAT THEY SEEM.

SHE'S IN THERE! WE HAVE TO GO NOW!
NO! WE MUST PROCEED WITH GREAT CARE.

WHY?
WHILE YOU WERE TALKING TO THE MEDIA PEOPLE, I WAS TALKING TO THE **WIZARD**.

YOU CAN **DO** THAT?
I CAN, AND HE HAS A WARNING FOR YOU. HE SAYS YOU ARE IN GRAVE **DANGER** . . .
REMEMBER THE PARADOX? THE **SHAZAM PARADOX**

NOT REALLY. . .
THEN I WILL REMIND YOU. NEVER SAY THE MAGIC WOR
WHILE AT THE **ROCK OF ETERNITY** BECAUSE "MAGIC WITHIN MAGIC" COULD CAUSE YOUR POWERS TO GO **OUT OF CONTROL**.
BECAUSE OF YOU **THOSE MONSTERS** MAY HAVE COME **THROUGH** THE ROCK O
ETERNITY. . .

SO? WHAT'S **THAT** GOT TO DO WITH ANYTHING?
THERE IS NO NEED TO BE **IMPATIENT**. I AM TRYING TO **EXPLAIN** - -

WE DON'T HAVE TIME!
BILLY--
WAIT!
SHAZAM!

CHAPTER 4:

NI NRMW NZPVH SRH NLEV!*

*THE MONSTER SOCIETY CODE

A	B	C	D	E	F	G	H	I	J	K	L	M	N	O	P	Q	R	S	T	U	V	W	X	Y	Z
Z	Y	X	W	V	U	T	S	R	Q	P	O	N	M	L	K	J	I	H	G	F	E	D	C	B	A

KA-BOOM!
BILLY, STOP!
LISTEN TO ME!
I CAN'T! I HAVE TO SAVE MARY!

IT'S CAPTAIN MARVEL!
WE'RE GOING TO NEED HELP OUT HERE!

CAPTAIN! WAIT!

COME BACK FOR MORE, DID YOU? GOOD!

POW!!

CRUNCH

THAT BOY NEVER LISTENS TO ME!

ROAR!

THANKS, TALKY TAWNY. WE GOT 'EM.
THIS IS BILLY BATSON'S IMPULSIVE BEHAVIOR - - NOT YOURS. GET CONTROL OF YOURSELF, CAPTAIN.
NOW LOOK OUT BEHIND YOU.

SOCK!

LET'S SEE WHAT'S INSIDE.
I DO NOT THINK THIS IS A GOOD IDEA.

A SECRET CHAMBER. SO THIS IS HOW THE MONSTERS CAME AND WENT SO QUICKLY...

WHAT'S THAT SMELL?

YEEEE!

WHO KNEW MONSTERS WERE SUCH POOR HOUSEKEEPERS?

NO SIGN OF MARY OR DR. SIVANA. . .
HMM.

A NARROW SHAFT. . .
IT LOOKS LIKE A PASSAGEWAY!
SIVANA MUST'VE ESCAPED THROUG THERE!

IT MIGHT BE A VENT OF SOME SORT - - BUT YOU'RE RIGHT, IT'S THE ONLY WAY INTO THE UPPER PART OF THE ROBOT.
IT'S TOO SMALL - -

NOT FOR SIVANA OR MARY. IF THEY CAN FIT, SO CAN I, . . .AS BILLY!
STAND BACK!
STOP!
IT'S A TRAP!

WHAT?
WILL YOU NEVER LISTEN?! COME OUTSIDE BEFORE YOU SAY ANOTHER WORD!

BUT SIVANA IS GETTING AWAY WITH MARY!
DID YOU FORGET THE SHAZAM PARADOX? YOU ARE IN GRAVE DANGER!

WHAT DANGER?
YOU CANNOT USE YOUR MAGIC WORD INSIDE THE **ROBOT**!

THE WIZARD SAID THAT RULE ONLY APPLIES AT THE **ROCK OF ETERNITY** BECAUSE MY POWERS COULD GO **HAYWIRE.**
YES, MAGIC WITHIN MAGIC IS UNPREDICTABLE AND COULD **KILL EVEN YOU**!
BUT REMEMBER, **MR. MIND** CAME HERE **THROUGH** THE ROCK OF **ETERNITY** - -

- - IT IS VERY LIKELY THAT THE SAME RULES OF SPACE AND TIME THAT APPLY INSIDE THE WIZARD'S **CAVE** APPLY INSIDE **MR. MIND'S MONSTER ROBOTS**!
IF YOU GO INSIDE AS **BILLY BATSON**, YOU HAVE TO **STAY** BILLY BATSON.

I HAVE NO CHOICE. ONLY BILLY CAN FIT THROUGH THAT **SHAFT.** SHAZAM!
BOOM!
WAIT! I'M COMING WITH YOU!

THEN **HURRY UP**!
FROM THIS MOMENT ON, YOU MUST NOT SAY **SHAZAM**, BECAUSE **NO ONE** CAN PREDICT WHAT WILL HAPPEN - -
LOOK OUT!

CLANG!
HOLY MOLEY!
TALKY TAWNY IS TRAPPED **OUTSIDE**!

. . . AND I'M TRAPPED **INSIDE.**
GULP.
MAYBE I WAS BEING A **LITTLE** IMPULSIVE . . .

HEY. . . WHAT'S **THIS?**

IT'S THE **GLOBAL POD.** I ALMOST FORGOT ABOUT IT!

I DON'T THINK IT WILL DO MUCH GOOD NOW THOUGH. HANG ON, MARY! I'M COMIN'!

HERE GOES NOTHING . . .

MAN, IT'S DARK IN HERE.

WOULD YOU LIKE SOME LIGHT, BILLY?
AAH!

DO NOT BE AFRAID--
I AM ONLY HERE BECAUSE OF YOU...
MR. MIND!!

DR. SIVANA WILL BE SURPRISED TO LEARN YOU ARE HERE...
WHERE IS HE? WHERE'S MARY?!

SEE FOR YOURSELF...
!

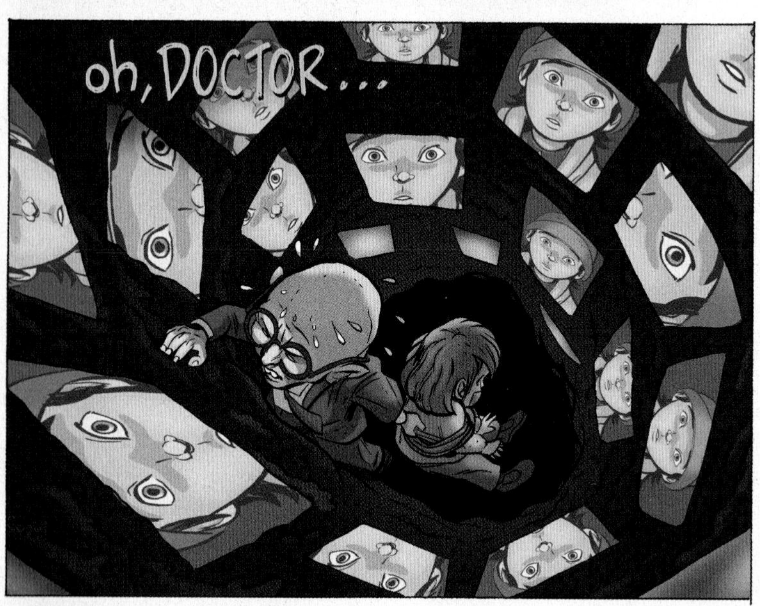
oh, DOCTOR...

EH?

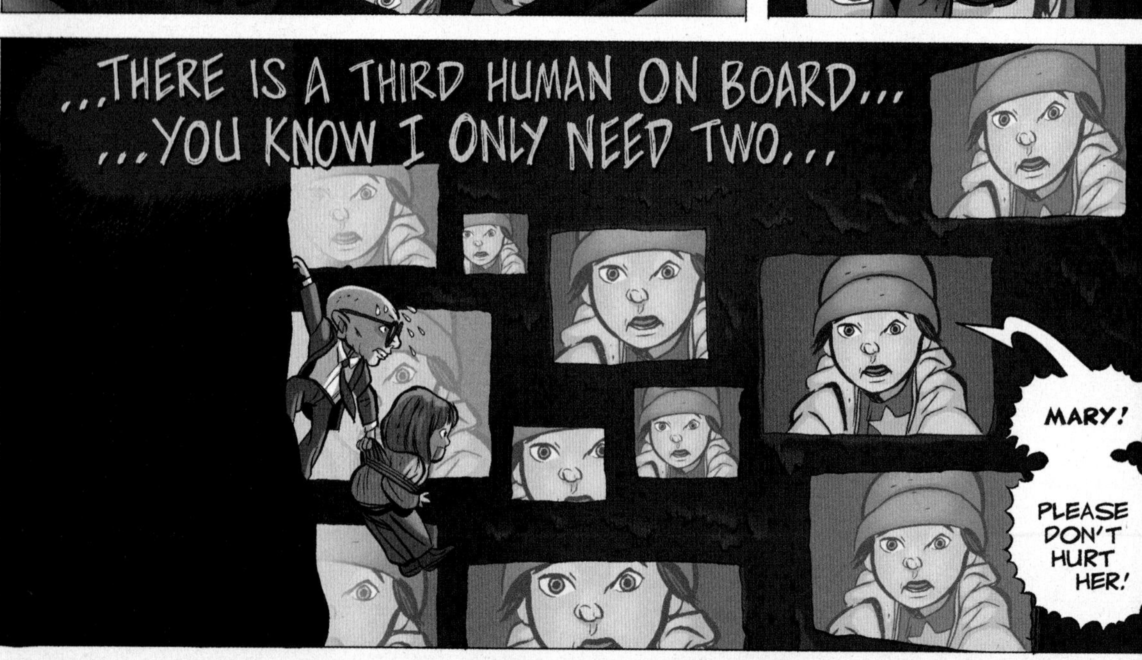
...THERE IS A THIRD HUMAN ON BOARD...
...YOU KNOW I ONLY NEED TWO...
MARY!
PLEASE DON'T HURT HER!

HE'S NOT WITH ME! LISTEN, MIND, I'M HOLDING UP MY END OF THE DEAL . . . YOU JUST HOLD UP YOURS!
Huff puff!
WHAT DEAL?

AND YOU BETTER GET RID OF BILLY BATSON - - THAT KID IS TROUBLE!
I DON'T KNOW WHAT TO DO . . .

WAIT! MAYBE THE GLOBAL POD CAN CONTACT HELEN FIDELITY!

WHAT'S THAT IN YOUR HAND, BILLY?
HELLO? CAN ANYBODY HEAR ME?

MR. MORRIS! SOMETHING IS COMING THROUGH!
FINALLY!
NO PRESS BEYOND THIS POINT
PRESS AREA

HELLO?
WHO IS THIS? WHERE IS CAPTAIN MARVEL?

MY NAME IS BILLY BATSON! I'M THE LITTLE KID WHOSE SISTER WAS KIDNAPPED BY ATTORNEY GENERAL SIVANA!

I KNOW YOU DON'T BELIEVE SHE WAS KIDNAPPED, BUT I'M INSIDE ONE OF THE GIANT MONSTERS NOW - - AND SIVANA IS UP ABOVE ME WITH MARY! I CAN SEE THEM ON TV SCREENS!

SHOW US, BILLY. POINT THE GLOBAL POD AT THE TV SCREENS.
SNAP! SNAP!

THERE! SEE? SIVANA HAS MARY - - AND SHE'S TIED UP!

SIR, I CAN'T QUITE MAKE OUT THIS PICTURE. . .
LET THE LAWYERS TAKE A LOOK.

BILLY, WE'RE HAVING A HARD TIME SEEING... TRY TO HOLD THE CAMERA STILL.
OKAY, HOW'S THAT?
CLK CLK CLK! ZZZT! ZZDT!

ALMOST... WE'RE PICKING UP A STRANGE BUZZING SOUND.
UM ...
I THINK THERE'S SOMETHING **MOVING** IN HERE.
CLK! CLK! ZZT!
ZZT! ZZZT!

CLK? CLK?
!

WHAT DO YOU THINK?
THE IMAGE IS TOO **BLURRY**. IT'S IMPOSSIBLE TO SAY IF THE ATTORNEY GENERAL IS **KIDNAPPING** THE LITTLE GIRL OR HELPING HER **ESCAPE**.

HELPING HER? IT LOOKS LIKE HE'S DRAGGING HER AGAINST HER WILL.
THAT'S YOUR INTERPRETATION. WE ADVISE YOU TO KEEP THIS **OFF** THE AIR.

RIDICULOUS! HELEN, PUT THIS ON THE AIR IMMEDIATELY!
SIR! THERE ARE TOO MANY QUESTIONS - -
MISS FIDELITY!

BILLY! WHAT'S WRONG?
I CAN ANSWER ONE QUESTION . . .

. . . I KNOW WHERE ALL THE COCKROACHES IN THE CITY WENT TO!
KLK!
KLK!
CAN YOU SEE THIS?
CLK!
TK! TK! TK!

EEERG - -
BILLY! CAN YOU HEAR ME? WHERE IS YOUR FRIEND CAPTAIN MARVEL?

AT THE FOOT OF THE ROBOT MONSTER YOU'LL FIND MY OTHER FRIEND TALKY TAWNY! - - HE CAN HELP ME - -

THE SIGNAL WENT DEAD!
GOOD LORD! WE HAVE TO TELL THE AUTHORITIES.

WE'VE GOT TO GO INSIDE THE PARK AND FIND HIS FRIEND TALKY TAWNY!
WE DON'T ADVISE THAT... OUR INSURANCE WON'T COVER IT.

THOSE CHILDREN HAVE BEEN KIDNAPPED!
ALLEGEDLY! MAY WE REMIND YOU BOTH THAT SIVANA INDUSTRIES, INC. IS THE WORLD'S LARGEST SUPPLIER OF MILITARY WEAPONS SYSTEMS?

WHAT ARE YOU GETTING AT?
THE GOVERNMENT MAY HAVE AN OPINION ABOUT THIS STORY...

MAY I REMIND YOU THAT WE STILL HAVE FREEDOM OF THE PRESS IN THIS COUNTRY, RIGHT, HELEN?
...HELEN?
NO PRESS BEYOND THIS POINT
PRESS AREA

CRUSH!
CRUSH!
CRUSH!
HUMAN! CRUSH THE HUMAN!

CRUSH!
CRUSH!
WAIT!
WHY WAIT?

THIS HUMAN ONCE SPARED MY LIFE.
WE SHOULD SPARE HIS.
BUT MR. MIND SAID WE MUST CRUSH **ALL** HUMANS!

CRUSH! CRUSH! CRUSH!
HUMAN! CRUSH THE HUMAN!
STOP! WE ALSO VOUCH FOR THIS HUMAN!
FREE HIM!

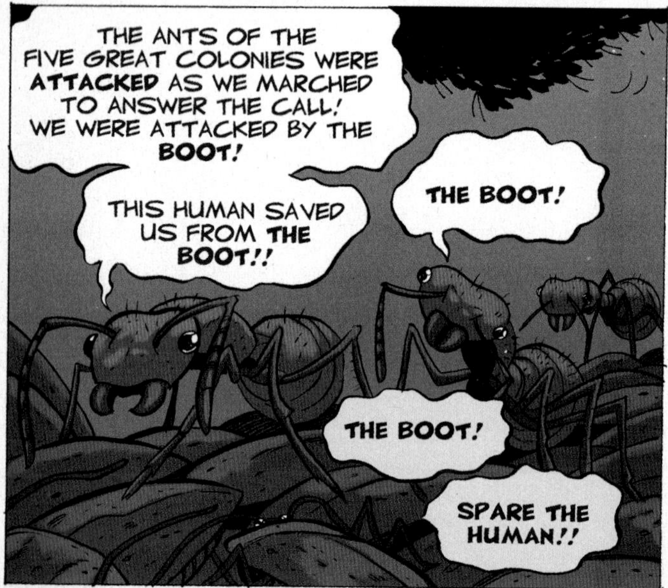
THE ANTS OF THE FIVE GREAT COLONIES WERE **ATTACKED** AS WE MARCHED TO ANSWER THE CALL! WE WERE ATTACKED BY THE **BOOT**!
THIS HUMAN SAVED US FROM **THE BOOT**!!
THE BOOT!
THE BOOT!
SPARE THE HUMAN!!

FREE HIM!
YES! FREE HIM!
GAA!

WHAT'S GOING ON?! WHAT ARE ALL YOU BUGS DOING HERE?!
WE WERE SUMMONED BY MR. MIND.
OUR MASTER HAS CALLED US!
WE HAVE COME TO DRIVE THE MACHINE!

WHAT DO YOU MEAN DRIVE THE MACHINE?
THE MACHINE WE ARE STANDING IN! IT IS A WAR SHIP SO POWERFUL THAT ALL THE CITIES OF THE EARTH WILL BE EXTERMINATED!

EVEN NOW OUR BROTHERS AND SISTERS ARE FILLING UP BOTH OF THE GREAT WAR SHIPS! WE SHALL DRIVE THE MACHINES AND CRUSH THE HUMANS!!
ALL WE ARE WAITING FOR IS THE ARRIVAL OF THE FINAL WAR SHIP - - THE DESTROYER!
AND IT COMES TONIGHT!!

I DON'T UNDERSTAND! WHY WOULD YOU DO THIS? YOU'LL WIPE OUT ALL CIVILIZATION!
NOT ALL CIVILIZATION. JUST HUMAN CIVILIZATION.
DRIVE THE MACHINE!

HUMAN CIVILIZATION PAVES OVER EVERYTHING!
HUMANS USE POISON GAS TO EXTERMINATE WHOLE COLONIES OF OUR KIND!

ATTENTION, BROTHERS AND SISTERS! THE HOUR OF TWO LIGHTS APPROACHES!
ESCORT BILLY BATSON TO THE COCKPIT...

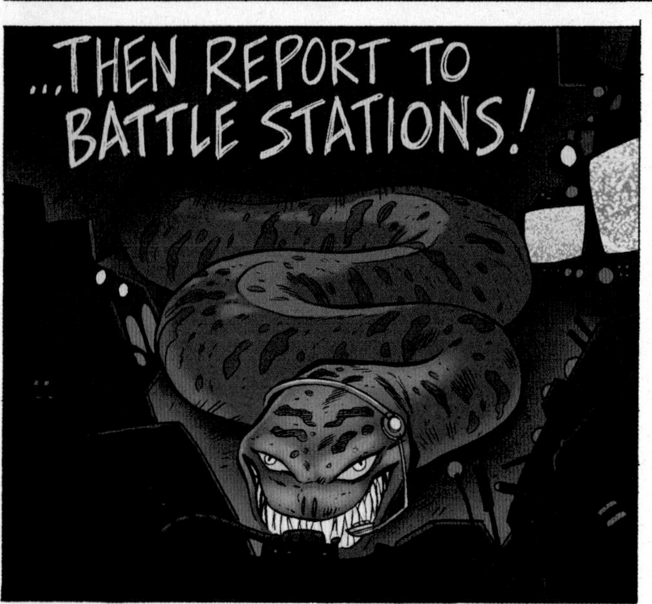
...THEN REPORT TO BATTLE STATIONS!

YOU HAVE BEEN SUMMONED BY THE GREAT MR. MIND HIMSELF! HURRY - - OUR MASTER DOES NOT LIKE TO BE KEPT WAITING!
GULP!

MR. MORRIS, CAN YOU HEAR ME? I'M INSIDE THE PARK AND READY TO GO ON THE AIR . . .
HELEN! ARE YOU SURE THIS IS SAFE?

OKAY, HELEN . . . GET READY TO
GO LIVE - - IN THREE, TWO - -

THIS IS HELEN FIDELITY REPORTING LIVE FROM INSIDE THE PARK NOT FAR FROM THE FEET OF MR. MIND'S GIANT MONSTERS!
SNN
HELEN FIDELITY

NOT LONG AGO, SNN RECEIVED A CALL FOR HELP FROM INSIDE ONE OF THE MONSTERS!
THE CALL CAME FROM A LITTLE BOY WHO CLAIMS HIS SISTER HAS BEEN KIDNAPPED!

ZZZCH!
MISS FIDELITY? IT'S ME, BILLY - -
DID YOU FIND MR. TALKY TAWNY YET?
BILLY!
WHERE ARE YOU?!!

I'M STILL INSIDE THE MONSTER ROBOT - - I MUST BE NEAR THE TOP BY NOW.
DR. SIVANA AND MARY CAN'T BE FAR AHEAD OF ME.
BILLY, WE ARE ON LIVE TV. CAN YOU DESCRIBE YOUR SURROUNDINGS?

WELL, IT SORT OF LOOKS LIKE A SPACESHIP, I GUESS . . .
BUT WITH BUGS.
DID YOU FIND MY FRIEND?

ONLY ON THE MONITORS, BUT I MUST BE CATCHING UP - - I'M ALMOST TO THE TOP...
BILLY, LISTEN TO ME VERY CAREFULLY...

RESCUE MARY AND COME BACK DOWN HERE AS QUICKLY AS POSSIBLE. YOU MUST NOT BE INSIDE THE ROBOT WHEN THE HOUR OF TWO LIGHTS ARRIVES!

HAT'S STRANGE...
I SHOULD BE ABLE TO SEE THEM BY NOW.
PLEASE, BILLY! REMEMBER THE PARADOX!
IF YOU DO NOT COME BACK OUTSIDE, CAPTAIN MARVEL WILL NOT BE ABLE TO HELP US!
DO YOU UNDERSTAND?

BILLY? ARE YOU LISTENING TO ME?
I'M LISTENING.
LOOK AT THE MONITORS - - SIVANA AND MARY ARE GOING THROUGH SOME KIND OF HATCH.

CLANK!
ERNF!

THERE YOU GO, BRAT.
MM!

YOU'RE PRETTY HEAVY FOR A LITTLE GIRL.

NOW, LET'S SEE WHERE WE ARE . . .
CLANG!

HEY! DO YOU GUYS SEE THIS? SIVANA AND MARY ARE ON TOP OF THE MONSTER ROBOT!
KLK! KLK!

GET SOME CAMERAS IN THE AIR! I WANT A CLEAR SHOT OF THIS!
SNN
WHIZ

ALL RIGHT, MR. MIND - - I BROUGHT THE GIRL TO THE TOP. NOW WHAT?

STRAP HER INTO THE COCKPIT!

OKAY, KID. LET'S GO!

FLASH!
WHAT TH - - ?

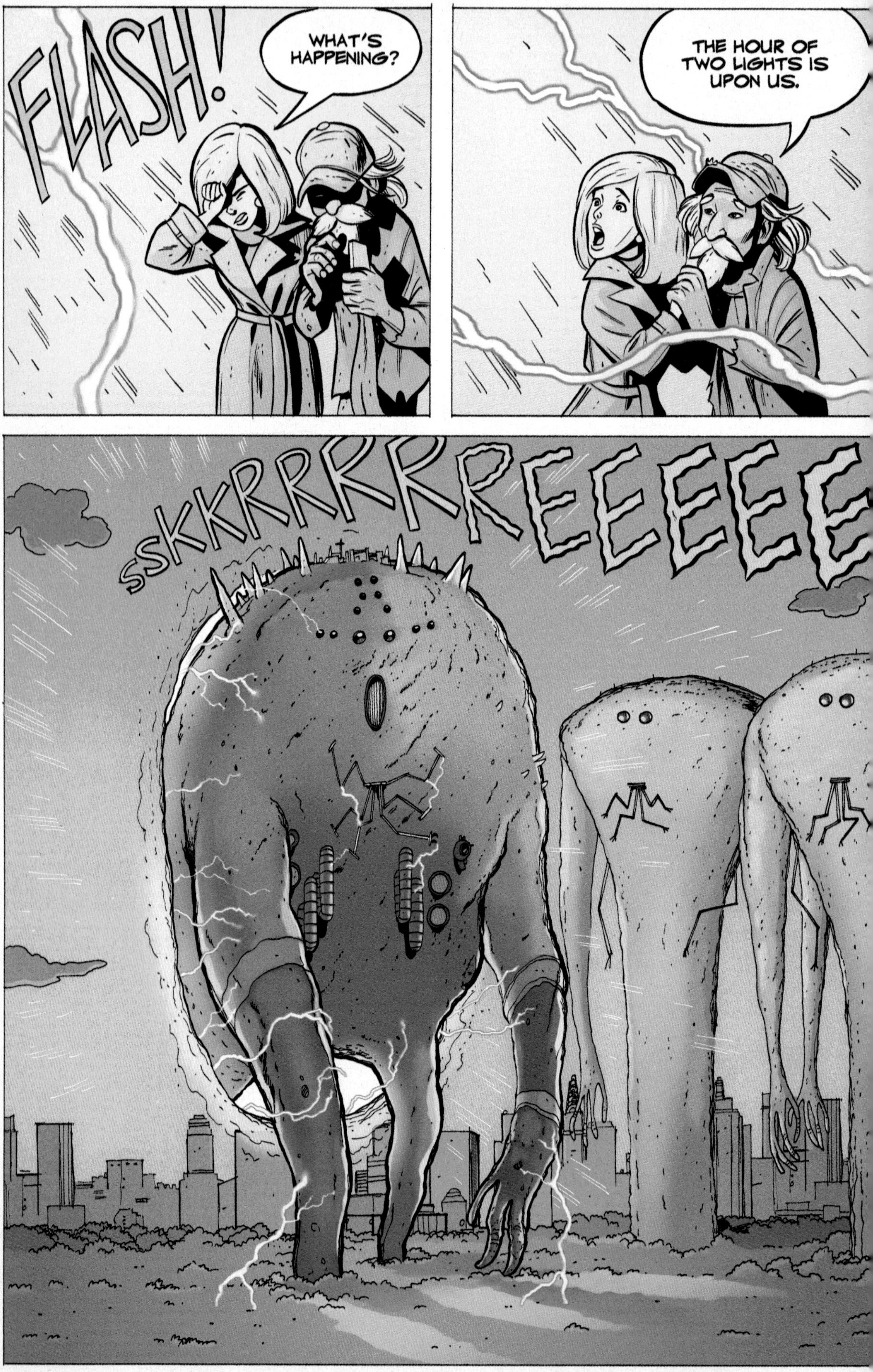

sSKKRRRRREEEEEE

BILLY -- THE FINAL COMPANION IS HERE!!
ZZRKT!
IT'S A WARSHIP CALLED THE DESTROYER! WE HAVE TO HURRY!
MR. MIND HAS TURNED THE INSECTS OF EARTH AGAINST US . . .

. . .THE INSECTS IN HERE ARE WAITING TO TRANSFER OVER TO THE DESTROYER SO THEY CAN COMMAND IT!
RRR!
I'VE REACHED THE HATCH, BUT IT'S STUCK!

BILLY, PLEASE COME DOWN! WITHOUT CAPTAIN MARVEL WE ARE DOOMED!
LOOK BEHIND US!

INSECTS ARE FLOODING OUT OF THAT GRATE!

THEY ARE ALL GOING OVER TO THE DESTROYER!
THIS IS HORRIBLE! WHERE'S THE ARMY? WHY AREN'T THEY BOMBING THAT THING?

-- HOLD YOUR FIRE. DO YOU UNDERSTAND ME?
THE MILITARY IS TO STAND DOWN UNTIL YOU HEAR FROM ME.
ROGER THAT.

THAT TAKES CARE OF THAT.
VERY GOOD.

NOW GET MARY INTO THE COCKPIT!
YEAH, YEAH. THIS BETTER BE WORTH IT!

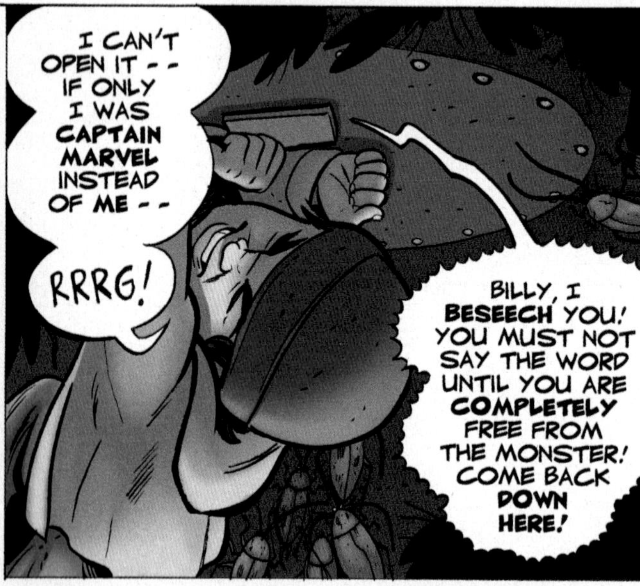
I CAN'T OPEN IT -- IF ONLY I WAS **CAPTAIN MARVEL** INSTEAD OF ME --
RRRG!
BILLY, I **BESEECH** YOU! YOU MUST NOT SAY THE WORD UNTIL YOU ARE **COMPLETELY** FREE FROM THE MONSTER! COME BACK **DOWN HERE!**

CLANK!
I GOT IT!

WAIT A MINUTE! THE COCKPIT IS **EMPTY!**
ACCORDING TO THE **MONITORS**, MARY AND SIVANA SHOULD BE **RIGHT HERE!**

HOLY MOLEY! SIVANA AND MARY WERE IN THE OTHER MONSTER THE WHOLE TIME! I WAS TRICKED!

WHAT'S GOING ON HERE? WHY IS THERE ONLY ONE SEAT IN THE COCKPIT? I THOUGHT YOU WERE GOING TO SHOW ME THE SECRETS OF THESE ASSAULT VEHICLES!
I WAS...

...BUT I ONLY NEED ONE HUMAN PER VEHICLE...
!
YOU ARE NO LONGER NECESSARY.

QUICK! GET IN THE COCKPIT, HUMAN!
YES! WE WILL SHOW YOU HOW TO MOVE THE MONSTER'S ARM, THEN YOU CAN REACH OVER TO YOUR SISTER!
OKAY!

BILLY, THIS IS HELEN! WHAT'S **GOING ON** UP THERE?

EVERYTHING'S OKAY! THE BUGS ARE TEACHING ME HOW TO **DRIVE THIS THING** SO I CAN **SAVE MARY!**

WHAT'S HAPPENING?!
SOME-ONE IS ON TOP OF THE **MONSTER!**
SIR, THE MILITARY WON'T LET US PUT CHOPPERS IN THE AIR - -
THEN GET A CAMERA ON TOP OF A **BUILDING! I WANT THIS SHOT!**
LOOK!
ONE OF THE CREATURE'S ARMS IS MOVING!!
SNN
DO NOT CROSS

WHAT ARE YOU TRYING TO **PULL**, MIND? YOU SAID YOU NEEDED **TWO** HUMANS.
YES... THE NERVOUS SYSTEMS OF EARTH INSECTS ARE NOT UP TO MY TASKS...
...WHEN WE MADE OUR DEAL, YOU AND THE GIRL WERE THE ONLY HUMANS I HAD...

BUT NOW THAT I HAVE TWO **MARVELS** TO DRIVE MY COMPANION MONSTERS, ALL MY NEEDS ARE SATISFIED...
KINDLY THROW YOURSELF OFF.

THROW MYSELF OFF?!!
GET BENT, MIND!

I'LL SHOW YOU WHAT I THINK OF YOUR MARVELS!
MM!
MM!

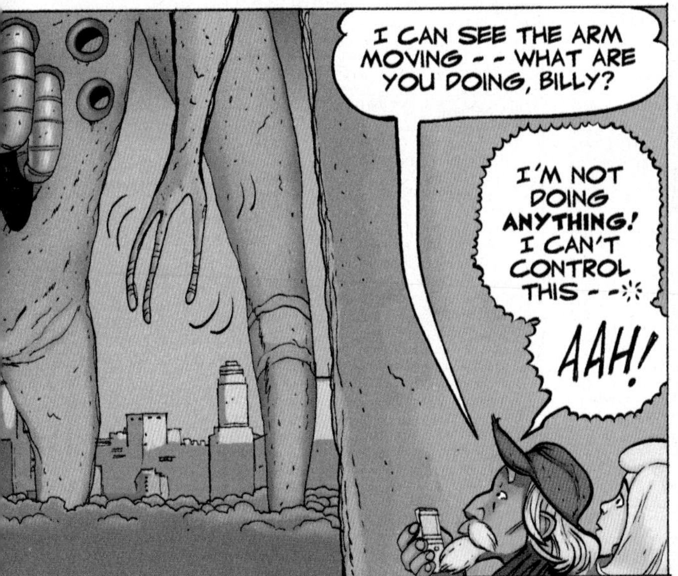
I CAN SEE THE ARM MOVING - - WHAT ARE YOU DOING, BILLY?
I'M NOT DOING ANYTHING! I CAN'T CONTROL THIS - -
AAH!

BILLY! WHAT'S WRONG?!
THE COCKPIT - -
GRK! IT'S STRANGLING ME!

AND THE ARM! IT'S COMING RIGHT FOR ME!
HA! HA! HA!

HA!
HA!
HA!

THANK YOU FOR THE USE OF YOUR NERVOUS SYSTEM, BILLY BATSON . . .

. . . THE ARM WILL NOW LIFT ME OVER TO THE COCKPIT OF MY WARSHIP THE DESTROYER!
HA! HA! HA!

YOU?! YOU'RE MR. MIND?!!
HA! HA!

YES, AND VERY SOON, ALL YOU GIANT, CLUMSY HUMANS WILL BE HISTORY!
HA! HA! HA!

HEY, MIND!
I GOT YOUR MARVEL!

LET'S SEE WHAT'S SO MARVELOUS ABOUT HER **NOW!**

HE THREW HER OFF! THE ATTORNEY GENERAL JUST THREW THE LITTLE GIRL **OFF THE MONSTER!** DID YOU GET THAT?!

DID WE GET THAT ON CAMERA?
WE GOT IT.
SNN

BILLY? THIS IS **TALKY** - - SIVANA HAS THROWN MARY FROM THE CREATURE! CAN YOU CONTROL THE ARM AND CATCH HER?

BILLY! CAN YOU HEAR ME? ISN'T THERE ANYTHING YOU CAN DO?

SHAZAM.

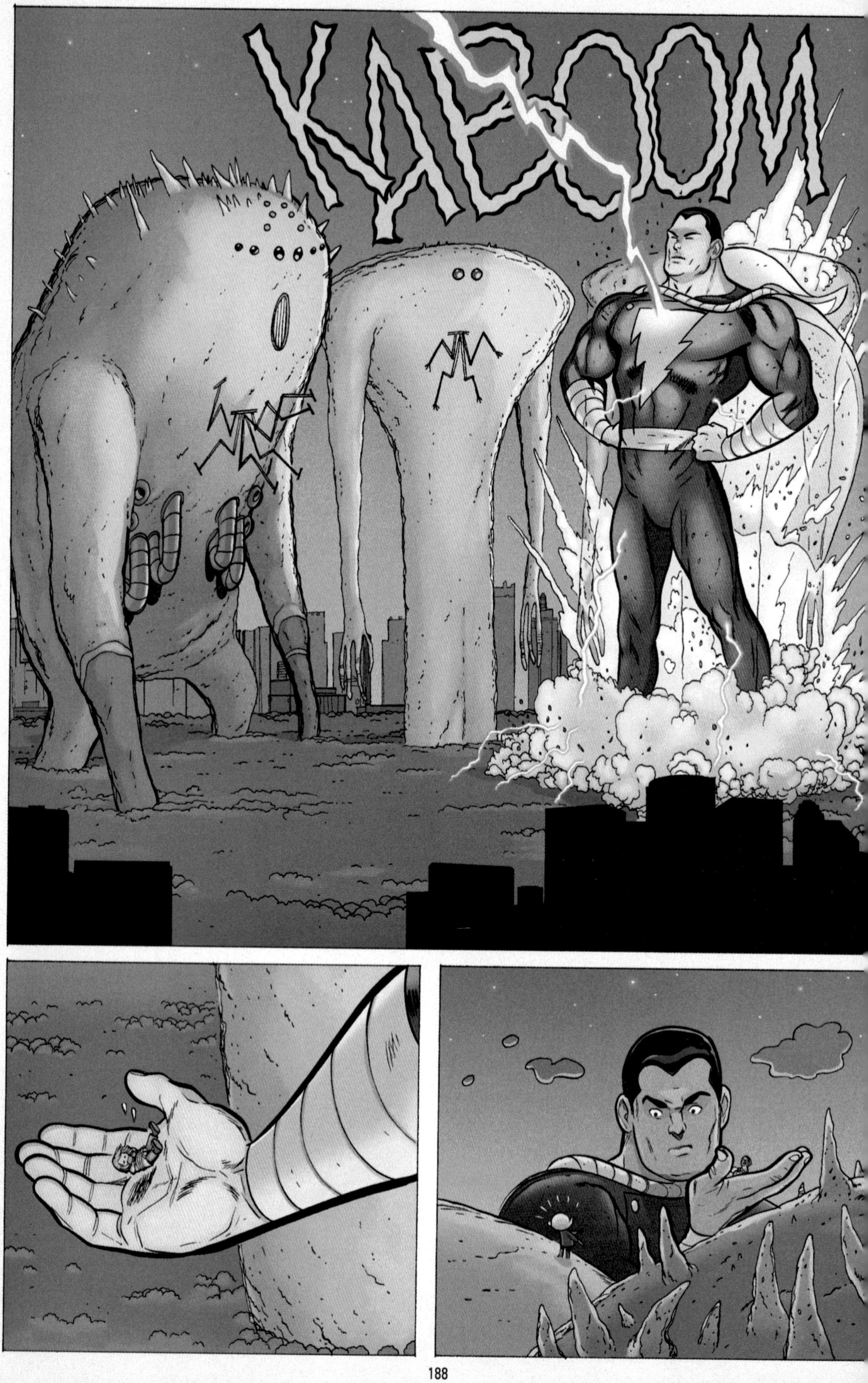

KABOOM

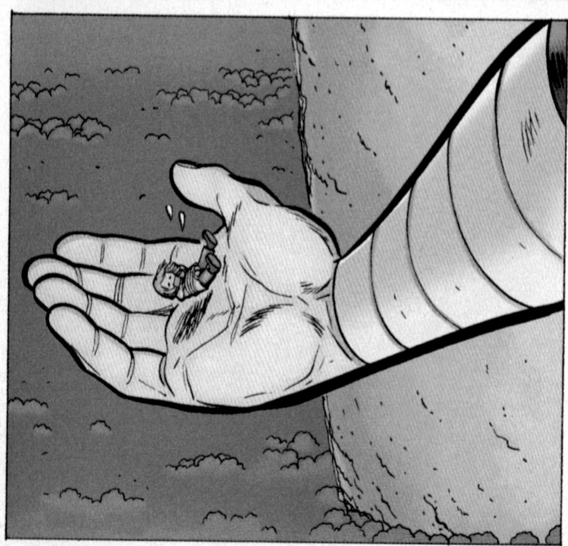

WHAT HAPPENED - - ?! oh--!
LOOK! THE INSECTS ARE ALL INSIDE THE DESTROYER!

SHHK!

KILL CAPTAIN MARVEL!

WOOOOOOOOOOOOO
HA HA HA!
CHUNK!
WHP! WHP!
CHNG!
WHP!
WHP!
WHP!
WHP!
CHNG!
CHNG

CRUNCH!
POW

LOOK OUT!

KRAK

POW

HE STILL HAS MARY IN HIS HANDS!
WATCH OUT FOR THE BUILDINGS!

HAHAHAHA!
CAN'T TAKE IT, EH?
GOOD.
WE'RE ABOUT TO RELEASE THE POISON.

IT'S TIME TO FUMIGATE THIS PLANET...

LAST CHANCE . . .
IS THAT ALL YOU'VE GOT, MARVEL?

STAY HERE.

HEY, MIND..
HOW ABOUT THE STRENGTH OF HERCULES . . .

WITH A LITTLE ZEUS BOOST!

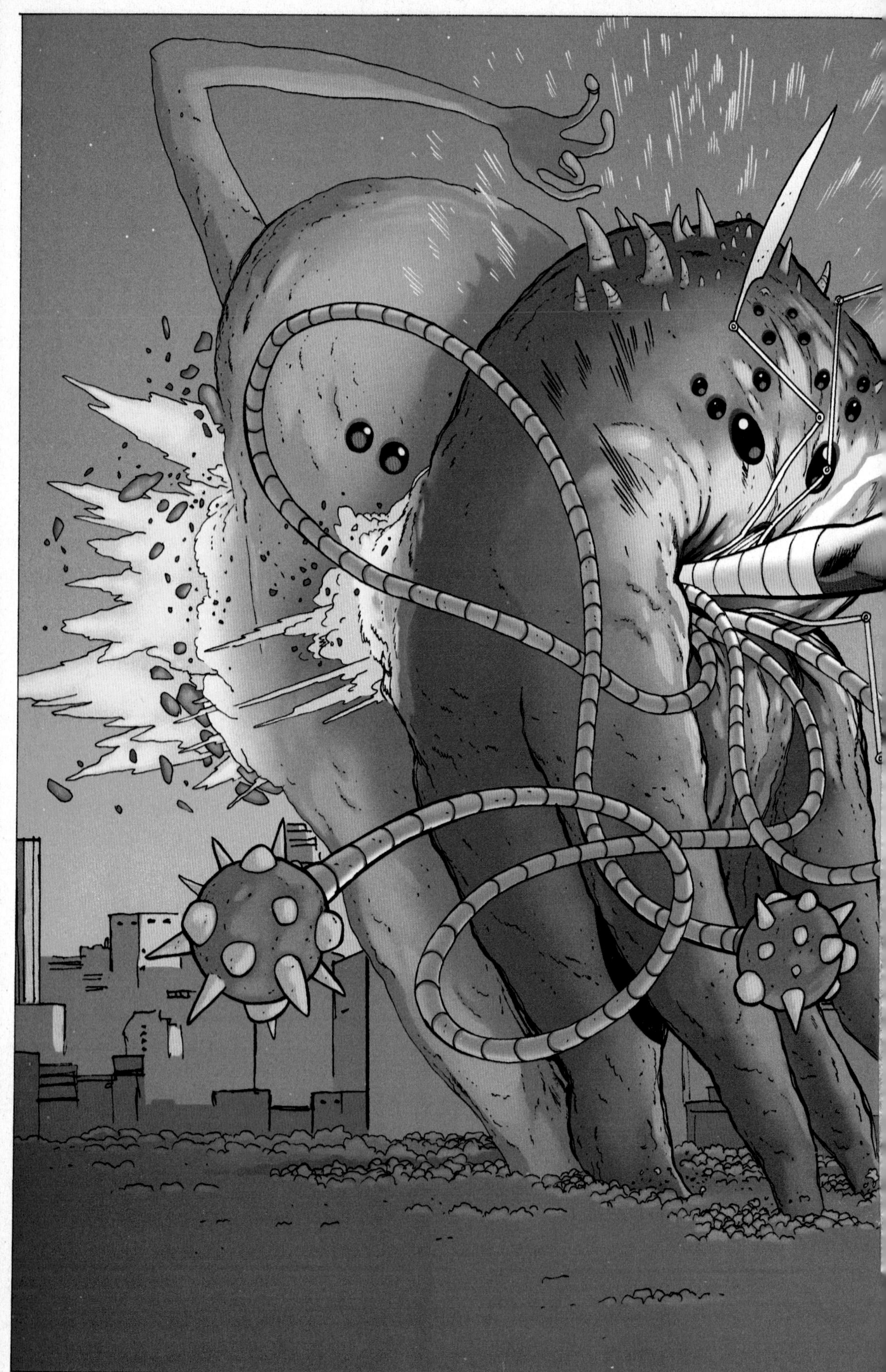

HOORAY!!!
SNN

GO, CAPTAIN MARVEL!!
OH, NO! THIS IS **VERY BAD!** CAPTAIN MARVEL PUNCHED HIM **TOO HARD!**

WHAT DID YOU SAY?
THE FABRIC OF LIGHT HAS BEEN COMPRESSED INTO A **SINGULARITY!** A SMALL **BLACK HOLE** HAS FORMED - -

AND IT IS PULLING EVERYTHING BACK TO **ETERNITY- -**
INCLUDING **CAPTAIN MARVEL!**

MARVEL--
WHAT HAVE YOU DONE TO US?!!

KRACK

LOOK, MR. TAWNY! BILLY AND SIVANA ARE ALIVE! THEY'RE PERCHED ON TOP OF THOSE TWO GIANT COLUMNS OF INSECTS!
MY GOODNESS! THAT IS A LOT OF COCKROACHES. . . WHAT IS HOLDING THEM UP?

OH, I SEE! NOTHING!

THIS IS GOING TO BE UN-PLEASANT!
. . .

GOOD LORD!
THE ROACHES ARE RETURNING TO THEIR HOMES ALL OVER THE CITY!
SNN

GAA!

THAT WAS GROSS!!
BILLY! WHERE'S YOUR SISTER?

TALKY! I LEFT HER TIED UP ON A BUILDING LEDGE!
QUICK! GO GET HER!

SHAZAM!

HEY-- I DIDN'T CHANGE!
TRY AGAIN!

SHAZAM! SOMETHING'S WRONG!
I WAS AFRAID OF THIS! WHEN YOU CREATED THAT SMALL BLACK HOLE, YOU NOT ONLY SENT MR. MIND BACK TO ETERNITY, BUT YOU SENT YOUR POWERS BACK, TOO!

WELL, ISN'T THAT INTERESTING.

I DON'T NEED POWERS TO THUMP YOU!

AHH!
UNCLE!
UNCLE!

THAT'S ENOUGH, BRAT!
BILLY! WATCH IT! HE'S GOT A GUN!

YOU FIRST, TIGER!
ROAR!

POW POW
ZZIIING!

WHEW!
I AM BULLET-PROOF!

NOW QUIT PLAYING WITH GUNS!
SLIP SLAP SLAP

MARY!
YOU'RE OKAY AND YOU STILL HAVE YOUR POWERS!

I WAS UP ON THAT LEDGE, BUT I FINALLY FREED MY HANDS AND PULLED THE TAPE OFF MY MOUTH!
YOU MUST HAVE BEEN FAR ENOUGH FROM THE SINGULARITY THAT YOUR POWERS ESCAPED!

HOLD MY HANDS, BRO.
YOU GAVE ME YOUR POWERS, MAYBE I CAN GIVE THEM BACK!
YOU THINK?

SHAZAM!
BOOM!

HEY, I'M BACK! MARY, YOU'RE A GENIUS!
I KNOW!
GOOD. NOW LET'S GET OUT OF HERE BEFORE THE ARMY ARRIVES!

SHAZAM!
BOOM!

I HATE YOU, YOU SNOTTY LITTLE..
POW!
POW!
POW POW!
FREEZE, KID-NAPPER!

DROP THE GUN!

WHO ARE THOSE THREE, REALLY?
WHO KNOWS, BUT I BET WE HAVEN'T HEARD THE LAST FROM THEM!

OR FROM ME.

AS YOU CAN SEE, BILLY, ALL THE EYES ON THE IDOLS ARE NOW CLOSED.

THE INTERESTING THING IS - -
MARY - - PLEASE STOP CLIMBING ON THE SEVEN DEADLY ENEMIES OF MAN. THANK YOU.

AS I WAS SAYING, THE INTERESTING THING IS THAT THE EYES CLOSED - - **NOT** WHEN CAPTAIN MARVEL VANQUISHED MR. MIND. . .

. . . BUT WHEN ATTORNEY GENERAL SIVANA WAS CAUGHT ON TAPE THROWING MARY OFF THE TOP OF THE MONSTER!
PRIDE

THAT MEANS **DR. SIVANA** WAS THE TRUE THREAT ALL ALONG!
WHAT ABOUT MR. MIND?

MR. MIND WAS DOOMED THE MOMENT SIVANA PROVOKED YOU INTO USING YOUR MAGIC WORD.
PERHAPS **FATE** WAS CONTROLLING OUR WORM-LIKE FRIEND THE WHOLE TIME. . . WHO KNOWS? THE FORCES OF ETERNITY ARE NOT ALWAYS EASY TO UNDERSTAND.

IN ANY CASE, HE IS **CONNECTED** TO YOU, BILLY. AND NOW THAT HE HAS HAD A TASTE OF OUR UNIVERSE, I'M SURE MR. MIND WILL BE **BACK**. WE MUST BE **ALERT**!

HE'LL HAVE TO GO THROUGH **US**, RIGHT, BRO?
RIGHT!
OH, HEY- - !

OH, MY **GOSH**! IT'S MR. MORRIS' **GLOBAL POD**! I FORGOT TO GIVE IT BACK!

BILLY BATSON, YOU HAD BETTER RETURN IT STRAIGHT AWAY!
I HAVE A FEELING MR. STERLING MORRIS WILL WANT TO HAVE A WORD WITH YOU, YOUNG MAN.

I WANT TO HAVE A WORD WITH YOU, YOUNG MAN.
MR. MORRIS

I KNOW. I'M SORRY I KEPT IT SO LONG. I **MEANT** TO GIVE IT BACK- -

GIVE IT BACK? SON! I WANT YOU TO **KEEP IT!**

YOU DO?
ARE YOU KIDDING? YOU AND HELEN WERE RATINGS **GOLD!** IN FACT, I WANT YOU TO COME WORK FOR US!

I WANT YOU TO BE A CORRESPONDENT AT THE FIRST STATION I EVER OWNED - - **W-H-I-Z** IN MIDTOWN. YOU'LL WORK RIGHT NEXT TO HELEN FIDELITY!

WE'LL BE **PARTNERS**, BILLY!
REALLY?
YOU WOULDN'T MIND WORKING WITH A LITTLE KID?

NOT IF YOU PUT IN A GOOD WORD FOR ME WITH YOUR FRIEND CAPTAIN MARVEL.
GULP.
OKAY.

WHAT DO YOU SAY, BILLY? WILL YOU BE PART OF THE WHIZ FAMILY?

BILLY?

WHAT'S WRONG?
I'VE NEVER BEEN PART OF ANY FAMILY BEFORE.

THAT SURE IS A BEAUTIFUL SUNSET...
YOU KNOW WHAT, BILLY? I THINK WE'LL BE ALL RIGHT.

YEAH, YOU'RE RIGHT!

THE MONSTER SOCIETY OF EVIL

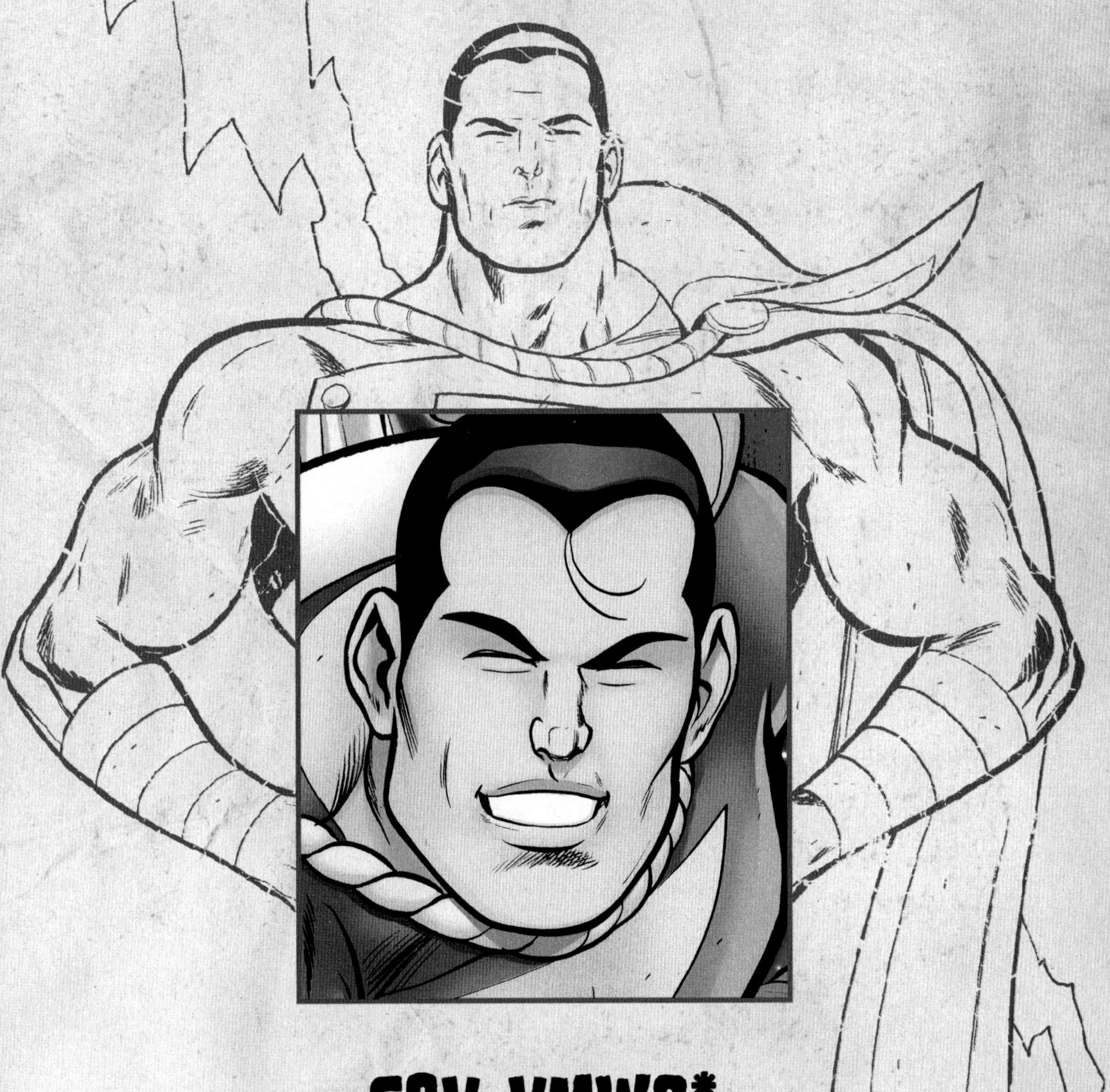

GSV VMW?*

***THE MONSTER SOCIETY CODE**

A	B	C	D	E	F	G	H	I	J	K	L	M	N	O	P	Q	R	S	T	U	V	W	X	Y	Z
Z	Y	X	W	V	U	T	S	R	Q	P	O	N	M	L	K	J	I	H	G	F	E	D	C	B	A

Jeff Smith

In 1991, Jeff Smith launched a company called Cartoon Books to publish his comic book *Bone*, a comedy/adventure about three lost cousins from Boneville. Against all odds, the small company flourished, building a reputation for quality stories and artwork. Word of mouth, critical acclaim, and a string of major awards helped propel Cartoon Books and *Bone* to the forefront of the comic book industry. In 1992, Jeff's wife Vijaya Iyer joined the company as partner to handle publishing and distribution, licensing, and foreign language publications.

In the spring of 2005, Graphix, an imprint of Scholastic Books, published a full color version of *Bone: Out from Boneville*, bringing the underground comic to a new audience and a new generation. Between projects, Smith spends much of his time on the international guest circuit promoting comics and the art of graphic novels. The Boneville travel blog can be found at boneville.com.